Timothy Arlott was born in London in 1950 and educated at Highgate School. After an unsuccessful attempt at making a living playing the banjo in the Faroe Islands, he started work at seventeen as a journalist on provincial daily newspapers. He later joined an international television news agency and has lived abroad for a number of years, notably in Japan, Australia, Iran and France. For the last four years he has lived in Paris with his wife Patricia and two children. He still dreams of making his living with the banjo, but perhaps not in the Faroe Islands.

John Arlott

A MEMOIR

———◆———

Timothy Arlott

PAN BOOKS

First published 1994 by André Deutsch Ltd

This edition published 1995 by Pan Books
an imprint of Macmillan General Books
Cavaye Place London SW10 9PG
and Basingstoke

Associated companies throughout the world

ISBN 0 330 33946 X

1 3 5 7 9 8 6 4 2

A CIP catalogue record for this book is available from the
British Library

Printed and bound in Great Britain by
Cox & Wyman Ltd, Reading, Berkshire

*To my father
in gratitude for his
unfailing love and humour*

Contents

———◆———

Acknowledgments

Apart from my heartfelt thanks to publishers HarperCollins for permission occasionally to quote from and use as reference my father's autobiography *Basingstoke Boy*, I am also indebted to David Rayvern Allen. David's painstaking transcripts of my father's broadcasts and compilations of his articles for magazines and newspapers for David's books *Arlott on Cricket*, *Arlott on Wine*, *A Word from Arlott* and *Another Word from Arlott* have saved much searching and the need to rely on a memory that may well have proved faulty. I am also grateful to the BBC for their permission to use part of David's transcript of the BBC radio interview my father did with the Surrey, Somerset and England cricketer Len Braund.

Finally I would like to thank my wife Patricia for her viciously efficient sub-editing and my agent Derek Wyatt, publisher Tom Rosenthal and editor David Wilson for their warming enthusiasm about this book which gave me the strength to see the project through.

Readers of my father's autobiography *Basingstoke Boy* may recognise some of the stories from his early life which I have also related here. I heard him tell all these stories many times, and since he told them so well it would have been absurd to try to improve on his own words. They are, I think, worth repeating.

Thanks to Patrick Eagar and the BBC for help with some of the photographs.

New Year 1965

Early on New Year's Eve 1965, my elder brother Jim switched off the TV programme my friend and I were watching and put on a record. He had asked us if we minded first. If it had been anyone else we might have minded but we were just 14 years old, he was 20, and treating us with politeness as well as humour despite the age difference was one of his many traits that gained our respect.

He put on Miles Davis's 'Porgy and Bess' – pretty complex stuff for 14-year-olds. He was drinking a cup of black coffee and reading the local evening paper, the *Southern Evening Echo*, which he worked for as a reporter. We listened to the record in silence. We had already heard him say in answer to my Dad's questions that he would be leaving after dinner because he had arranged to meet some chorus girls after a show in Southampton with some reporter friends. Being at an all-boys school, my friend David Law and I were still living on tales from our first mixed party at David's house some two months before and we were definitely impressed.

At the end of one side of the record Jim went up to get changed. David picked up his guitar and we went back to singing falsetto harmonies louder and louder to 'In the Pines, In the Pines'. At least David was singing falsetto harmonies because his voice had begun to break. I was doing my best to force mine to go the same way.

The meal with my father, stepmother Valerie, Jim and David was warm and friendly. Jim said goodbye and Happy New Year and went out to his sports car in the back yard. We all went on chatting but New Year's Eve meant very little to my father as a celebration. He preferred long dinner parties and conversation. I cannot envisage him holding hands with strangers singing 'Auld Lang Syne'. If he were up at midnight on New Year's Eve he would raise his wine glass and say 'Happy New Year, m'dears'.

That year he and Valerie went to bed around 11 p.m. David and I lay nattering in our twin beds in the bedroom at the end of the corridor. We were too old to find it exciting to stay up until midnight and – to our regret – too young to be invited to parties with girls lasting into the small hours.

Presently we fell asleep. For the first time in my life I woke up very late in the night and was unable to get back to sleep. I knew with a certainty I cannot explain that my brother had not returned to the bedroom next to ours. I wanted to hear the gravel crunch as his car swung into the back yard but I had a presentiment it would not be coming back.

After about an hour a car did swing into the back yard, its blue revolving light reflected through the net curtains on that side of the house. I reasoned to myself with frightening clarity that if Jim had been injured in a crash the police would have telephoned to say come to the hospital; if he had been stopped for a traffic offence there would be no reason for a police car to come to our home.

The policeman did not ring the bell. He managed to get in quite easily the way police can, although the back door was locked. I could hear his footsteps coming down the corridor towards our bedroom. He opened the door without turning on the light but I could just make out his face from the beam of the torch he was carrying. He shone it in my direction. He was in his fifties and you could tell he had broken news like this before, although his manner was neither automatic nor lacking in sympathy. 'Where does your Dad sleep, son?'

'Through the glass door down the other end of the corridor.'

David was awake now but neither of us said anything. After a minute my father's footsteps came fast down the corridor. He was in his pyjamas and his face was white. He went round the end of my bed and was oblivious to my questioning look.

'Jim's dead,' he said. He laid his head on my chest for a few seconds and then went back to his bedroom.

The Arlotts

This is a biography of a man who rose from being a clerk in a Hampshire mental hospital to the best known broadcaster in the land. He had a photographic memory; could charm the pants off a rattlesnake; was the best story-teller and most diverting company you could ever meet; a talker, listener, enthusiast, funny, lovable, shrewd and wise beyond credit; who got divorced, lost his eldest son, young wife and a baby in successive and terrible blows and became – partly because of these blows and two strokes – a selfish, demanding, limited and impossible old man. This is no objective biography. To me no man as large will ever walk the earth because he is my father, but those who knew him in his prime are unanimous that his was an enormous and memorable personality.

He died on 14 December 1991, but the best part of him died some fifteen years earlier.

To his admirers he was the finest cricket commentator there has been, with a sharply observant and humorous mind, a gift for language and an emotive voice.

To his friends he was richly rewarding – usually armed with a new amusing or gripping anecdote and a bottle of claret (he kept a bottle of claret and several glasses in his briefcase when travelling the cricket circuit) but ever ready to listen and possessing an impressive mind. He had his own habits, of course, but his responses were rarely predictable. He was great fun.

Beneath these two personae was an obsessive family man who had an amazingly happy second marriage but who was changed and increasingly broken by each successive death.

He left it too far into the twilight of his skill and years to write his own autobiography. As with most old people the memory of his early years was strong, but everyone I know who has read his autobiography, *Basingstoke Boy*, has asked the same questions – why does the narrative stop in the 1950s, before his divorce from my mother in 1959, and why does it mention only as a postscript the deaths of my brother and stepmother Valerie? The reason is simple. The only thing declining mental powers did for my father was to blunt the edge of those three deadly pains. No incentive made it worth bringing back the time and the demons. He could not bear to relive those wounds.

The Arlott clan come from the Hampshire/Berkshire border and most of them have not got much further. There are still no Arlotts in the London telephone directory but nearly a dozen in the Reading one. Our branch of the family – my father's grandfather, the furthest back the family memory goes – comes from Silchester. It is a little disappointing as a village unless you are a Roman archaeologist. The common is flat and scrubby and great-grandfather had a cottage on the edge of it. He was a seaman most of his life. His idea of hanging a picture was to drive a six-inch nail through the wall, and when in his seventies he went to see my grandparents in the 1923 Christmas of blizzards he ignored all entreaties to stay and walked the eleven miles back home through the drifts. It was time to go home: like my father, a man of definite opinions.

William the Conqueror was the bastard son of Robert of

Normandy and Arletta of Falaise, a tanner's daughter as my father used to tell me when I complained that our ancestry never seemed to rise above thieves, soldiers and grave-diggers. According to an encyclopaedia of name derivations, if derived from the French, Arlott means 'vagabond' or 'rogue' and if from ancient English 'a common labourer'. There is a Burgundy wine called Clos d'Arlot. My father dropped in there once hoping for a discount on a case or two, but word of cricket had not reached deepest Burgundy and the occupiers seemed singularly unimpressed by the idea of having English cousins; or perhaps they found my father's Hampshire French a bit of a strain.

My father had to buy the Annual Register for 1774. An entry helps explain why the Arlott clan is not more numerous. It reads:

> Winchester March 20. This day for robbing and threatening to murder D. Chase near Basingstoke, Robert Arlott was executed here pursuant to his sentence. He confessed the fact. His father and grandfather were both hanged here for offences of the like nature; his mother was transported; his brother is now here under sentence of deportation and he himself was tried at Reading on four indictments two years ago.

An ancestor fought in the Crimean War, and on his return to Silchester the lady of the Manor erected a marquee on the common to give the local soldiery a homecoming lunch. In the unaccustomed role of waitress, her ladyship was heard to observe after serving our ancestor, 'Only a common soldier and he wants salt.'

Apart from those transported to Australia, a great uncle Frank went there voluntarily but returned after about twenty-five years. After a number of enquiries he was directed to his brother Bert, who was working a field on a farm between Basing and Old Basing. Frank leant on the fence at the end of the field in line with the furrow Bert was ploughing. When Bert and the horse and plough reached the end of the furrow the two brothers looked each other in the eye for the first time in twenty-five years.

''Lo, Bert,' said Frank.

''Lo, Frank,' said Bert, turning the plough round and heading up the next furrow. Some minutes later he reached the end of the parallel furrow down by the fence.

'You'm be looking for work, I s'pose?' Bert ventured.

Frank agreed he was. Again the horse and plough turned and Bert continued the next furrow in contemplative mood. He returned several minutes later.

'There's plenty about,' he said.

My father's mother, Ellen 'Nellie' Clarke, was one of twelve children of an engineer of Scottish extraction who lived in a pleasant little housing estate called Meads village on the Beachy Head side of Eastbourne. She met my grandfather when she went to buy a coal shovel in the ironmonger's store in Meads village where he worked.

My grandfather had come to Eastbourne via the unlikely route for a Basingstoke boy of Harrods in Knightsbridge. He had gone to London looking for work; Harrods were impressed that grandfather seemed to know how to repair all things metal. Unfortunately my grandfather was impressed when a salesman in the hardware department called Parker asked him to go down to Eastbourne with him and be the repair man in an ironmonger's shop he was opening.

Fresh in love and completely in the dark about any financial problems Mr Parker might be having, grandfather turned up for work one day to find the shop locked. Mr Parker had gone bankrupt. There was no thought of leaving Nellie. They were married in 1913 and out-of-work Jack took the natural step for those days of returning home to

Basingstoke with his bride in the hope that his family might be able to find him something.

Jack's father, 'Old Jack', had left the sea by dint of finding work as the registrar at Basingstoke cemetery. As a local newspaper reporter in Basingstoke some sixty years later, I was startled awake to hear Councillor Harold Jackson, an old man and the only local at a winter's night committee meeting, mention my great-grandfather while discussing vandalism at the cemetery.

'When old Jack Arlott ran that cemetery no one entered who did not have a friend or relative buried there,' said Councillor Jackson. 'Anyone thinking of using the footpath as a short cut – let alone thinking of vandalism – was turned away in no uncertain terms.'

Old Jack was a tough little man covered in tattoos, unlike his son Jack who was a much more gentle character. In 1913 grandfather was very glad his father was cemetery registrar because he managed to install him and his new wife in the cemetery lodge. The building was an unlikely Swiss-style gatehouse on the Reading Road, but it gave the family a roof over their heads when grandfather went away to the war. My father was born there in February the following year and grandfather was called up in early 1915.

Jack served in one of those forgotten battlegrounds of the Great War – Mesopotamia, now Iraq. He played the trombone and most other wind instruments, so he was put in the band. He was a softly spoken, unwarlike man who contributed little to the defeat of Kaiser Bill. One of his four sisters, Edie, had nowhere to live when her husband was called up, so Old Jack billeted her in the cemetery lodge with Nellie. Thus my father, an only child, had the undivided attention of two women during his formative years. It gave him an expectancy of attention that neither he nor anyone around him would be likely to forget, especially in his later years. Not that Nellie spoiled unthinkingly, far from it. She was intuitive and observant

8

of her family with a humorous twinkle in her eye, but she had a sharp and worldly mind for a working-class house-wife. She dug the vegetable patch in the back garden herself and made sure my father could read by the age of four.

Simply getting the soldiers back from those far-flung warfronts was a difficult job, so it was a full year after the end of the war in 1919, when my father was five, that he first consciously saw his father.

Nellie was not an emotional woman, but going down to Basingstoke station every day as the troop trains came up from Southampton with the units that served in Iraq and returning home disappointed was a trauma which would transmit itself to any 5-year-old boy. One day Jack did appear, craning out of the carriage window. They turned and ran down the platform through the crowd. At once he was out of the train and clutching them both in his arms. His mates whom he would never see again – most of them being brass players from the north of England – threw his kitbag onto the platform for him. All three – Nellie, Jack and their son – were in tears as they left the station and headed up the Reading Road hill to home.

You can be sure there was no sudden injection of discipline into family life; any discipline came from Nellie. Jack was a loving, sentimental, soft father. If there was tension in the house or a row brewing he would go for a long walk hoping things would be better on return, so for Dad his father's homecoming just meant more love and attention in an already secure and happy household.

It was the year his father returned, even before he went to school at the age of six, that my father began his lifelong passion for collecting, starting with a booklet that was given away free with the comic *Rover*. He would even collect 'confetti', the punchings of the local bus conductors, before starting zealously keeping books – at first in an old boot box.

The following year, 1920, his parents sent him to the school his father had attended, Fairfields. Forty years later he bought a terraced house for his mother a rock's throw from the school in Beaconsfield Road. More importantly for his future, May's Bounty, Basingstoke's cricket ground, lay immediately behind the school.

One summer afternoon he and some other boys heard noises coming from the ground and, going to investigate, saw men in white hitting a hard ball in a net. His father said this was cricket and, being a practical man, he made my father a cricket bat. He bowled underarm at his son, but swimming was grandfather's sport and there was no sign of any Bradmanesque genius in his enthusiastic, chubby son.

The teachers at Fairfields were pleased with their bright, keen pupil, but one day my father was introduced to the contrary feminine world. He was showing the grass snake in his pocket to his school friends when a pretty red-haired teacher called Miss Tregarthen stormed up.

'Give me what you're playing with,' she demanded.

He did not think she would enjoy the grass snake but such a direct command could not be disobeyed. He was sent to the headmaster to receive two strops on each hand.

My father loved his childhood with his parents but books added an extra dimension – a free exploration of other worlds a country boy could never hope to know. On winter nights after tea and homework he would take a cup of cocoa and a candle upstairs to the long and narrow lead-windowed room in the bizarre cemetery lodge and read until the candle went out. His first adult books were by John Buchan and Jerome K. Jerome.

His father, who made most of the furniture in the house, made shelves for Dad's books and his mother a stiff cloth fringe for a cover. Nellie read a lot herself and was interested in politics. She joined the local women's Liberal association, became a delegate to the national conference and, exceptionally for a woman at the time, local election agent. I can sing 'Father knew Lloyd George' with conviction because my grandmother was in charge of arrangements when he came down to speak for the local Basingstoke candidate. He patted my father on the head on the railway platform and had tea in the house before Nellie took him round on his speaking engagements.

My grandparents were proud when Fairfields school told them they would be putting my father in for a scholarship to the county school a year early, but temper tantrums accompanied the strain of learning all the required material. There was one spectacular tantrum at home. My father had taken it upon himself to dig a hole in the garden to hide his saved pennies, but when he needed them he could not find where he had buried them. Nellie looked on in helpless mirth as his temper and frantic digging became ever more furious. When sleepless nights were added to tantrums, in a sign of my father's burgeoning dramatic hypochondria a mini 'nervous breakdown' was diagnosed – treated with Ovaltine and other 1920s remedies. It was part of the new faith in science of his Edwardian parents which Dad carried through his life that no matter what was wrong, some instant miracle remedy was available. To be kinder to my father's 'nervous breakdown', a friend from schooldays, Jack Donovan, remarked perceptively many years later that it was hard to realise how highly strung my father was because it was so well camouflaged. People who knew him as an adult would certainly not have guessed. He appeared relaxed and in command and was always more than able to defend himself in argument, but within the home it was clear that he was surprisingly thin-skinned, even a little hysterical over any personal insult.

The following year there were no such jitters when the school put him forward for two scholarships – the County Grammar School and the Aldworth Charity, a religious scholarship providing an extra pound towards school books.

The Bishop of Winchester's chaplain took the religious examination, which ended with an oral test. One of the set books was the Book of Common Prayer. My father handled the questions swiftly and the chaplain became interested.

'Where does this come from? – "Thou art a merciful God, full of compassion, long-suffering and of great pity. Thou sparest when we deserve punishment and in Thy wrath thinketh upon mercy."'

'A commination Denouncing God's Anger and Judgements against Sinners, sir.'

'"Are you persuaded that the Holy Scriptures contain sufficiently all doctrine required of necessity for eternal salvation through faith in Jesus Christ?"'

'Service for the Ordering of Priests, sir.'

'Do you know the entire prayer book by heart, young man?'

'Most of it, sir.'

He won both scholarships and the first 'highly commended' in religious knowledge in the Aldworth Examination for many years.

The County School was Queen Mary's Grammar School, a three-storey building in Worting Road that is now a technical college. Discipline was harsh and my father with many others conceived a hatred for the headmaster, Charles Percivall, whom he convinced himself was Prussian because his middle name was Wilhelm.

Percivall was a bad-tempered asthmatic who allegedly enjoyed caning and carried a cane as thick as his thumb in a hem of his cloak so that he would never be caught short. Masters would send a boy out of the classroom for a misdemeanour to see the headmaster at the washbasins where the beatings took place.

Most people retain both an abiding hatred of one schoolteacher and the deep friendships with schoolmates which the pressures of adolescent life intensify, and my father had plenty of friends. There were only 120 boys at the school and cricket was now not a matter of watching men in the nets at May's Bounty and occasionally being allowed to field. There was a school cricket pitch and regular games.

His best friend was another only child, John Carter. John shared my father's passion for reading and his love of sport. At cricket they would open the innings for house and school, and they would consider an excellent evening one where they sat in the same room, their heads buried in books which they would swap when finished.

John Carter died a few years ago. Another friend who endured a lifetime was Jack Donovan, an Irish Catholic as the name suggests though you would not have guessed it from his Basingstoke accent. Jack was more extrovert and gregarious than John Carter and surprisingly athletic despite his mighty frame. He would also amaze Dad with his party trick of being able to write two different preps simultaneously with a pen in each hand. He was ambidextrous.

Jack remembered my father as talkative; grand company; intelligent with an enquiring mind.

'He was always in trouble because he refused to compromise and used to query the teachers' decisions. He did not do it rudely but teachers were not prepared to be questioned in those days.

'I remember one occasion when John asked the science teacher Fairley Smith why you saw black spots in clusters when you shut your eyes. I thought it was rather an interesting question because I had often wondered that myself, but Fairley Smith said, "That's typical of you, Arlott, always trying to waste time."'

The teacher whose remarks most hurt my father was the English teacher, W. H. 'Boney' Pearce. Apart from reading most evenings, my father was keen to write. Holding aloft one of Jack Donovan's essays and one of my father's, Pearce said, 'Donovan, you will make a living with your pen; Arlott, I don't know why you bother.'

Jack recalls, 'Even at the time I thought he was barmy. I liked English and liked to think my essays were quite good, but I knew John's were better.'

Jack joined the Great Western Railway and was for many years one of British Rail's senior negotiators with the unions, so words did become a tool of trade even if they were not written. The pupil who should not have bothered had some eighty books and booklets published on cricket, wine, cheese, topography and poetry and wrote for quality national newspapers for more than thirty years.

Jack and my father enthused about all the sports played at Queen Mary's except cross-country. Dad used to say he could never see the point in running unless there was a ball in front of you or a purpose. Both he and Jack were too burly for cross-country, but like most large athletic people they could run short distances fast. They liked their housemaster and it was important to finish to get points for the house, so they would run a chequer-board race. With teachers, parents and spectators around the start they would sprint until out of sight when they were invariably up with the leaders. They had taken apples with them and they then would stroll along the undulating cross-country route north of Basingstoke talking of this and that until the route came back on to town streets, when they would sprint down the Worting Road and across the school playing fields to the crowd at the finishing line. They would finish around thirty-fifth of the sixty competitors, but to their great amusement in their mad half-mile finishing burst they would overtake less athletic boys who had diligently run the whole course.

While my father was at Queen Mary's, grandfather took over from Old Jack as cemetery registrar and the family moved into the new lodge in Worting Road. Holidays consisted of swapping the new lodge for Uncle Frank's flat in London or cycling nearly a hundred miles to my father's grandmother's house in Eastbourne.

Uncle Frank's flat was in Warwick Way in Pimlico – handy for my grandfather to get to the music hall and for Dad to get to the Oval. To his great excitement one of their early stays at Uncle Frank's coincided with the deciding England v. Australia Test Match of 1926. Well before the holiday he began cajoling his parents to let him go despite the large crowds predicted.

He had never seen Test players in the flesh before, but his avid reading and enthusiast's retention of facts armed him with an array of useless information. He informed the unfortunates around him as the Australian fast bowler, Gregory, opened the bowling that it was Gregory's thirty-first birthday. Two men then heroes, later to become friends, were playing for England – Jack Hobbs and Maurice Tate.

Since there had been no result in the preceding four Tests it had been decided that this one would be played to a finish. On that first day England were put out for 280, but Larwood, bowling faster than my father had seen anyone bowl, had Australia 60 for 4 at the close. His parents laughed kindly at his attempts to persuade them to let him see two more days' play, but the reality of Test cricket surpassed even his frenzied expectation and he was hooked.

He had to wait a year to fulfil his desire to see a whole game – on holiday with Grandmother Clarke at Eastbourne where Sussex were playing the County champions, Lancashire. Lancashire appeared on the run-in to be likely champions again but with the morning sea air giving the Sussex fast bowlers conditions they knew well how to exploit, 'Tishy' Browne, a schoolmaster from St Andrew's School behind Grandma's house, broke through. McDonald replied in kind for Lancashire when Sussex batted, but Holdsworth and Arthur Gilligan put on 188 for the eighth wicket.

Lying near the sightscreen, Dad watched Maurice Tate's swing and movement off the pitch as he and Browne went through the Lancashire batting cheaply again to give Sussex victory by an innings. It was a defeat which looked to have cost Lancashire the championship, but the sense of theatre in cricket for a sport-obsessed boy was provided by the Lancashire captain Leonard Green's generous speech at the end congratulating Sussex.

By the last match of the season Nottinghamshire needed only to beat Glamorgan, who had not won a game all season, to take the championship. Yet to the astonishment of all cricket followers Nottinghamshire lost by an innings and Lancashire won the championship. To a boy following the scores avidly in the morning paper it seemed like divine justice because of Green's gracious words.

Football was also a passion, spurring many a 17-mile bicycle ride to Reading with Jack Donovan or other sports-mad school friends. In 1926-27 George Camsell of Middlesbrough had broken the League goal-scoring record, so it was decided when Reading played Middlesbrough the following season that Camsell must be studied. It did not take the agents from Queen Mary's school long to work out how he was doing it. He hung just onside by the two full backs (centre-halves played well forward in those days) and waited for Jackie Carr to slip the ball through, then sprinted on to it as the backs turned and belted it past the advancing goalkeeper.

My father had by now shed his puppy fat and was big and lusty. He and Jack Donovan worked this football trick for their remaining school years at house level and eventually for the school. Dad played Camsell, hovering around up front while Jack stroked the ball through. All went well and many sides were beaten until they came to play their arch rivals, Peter Symonds of Winchester.

Peter Symonds was not only a much bigger school than Queen Mary's, it had a coach. Either he had also seen Middlesbrough, the school's backs were faster and more alert, or both. Peter Symonds were leading 7–0 halfway through the second half when the ever enthusiastic if frustrated centre-forward Arlott followed up a forlorn through ball that was already in the goalkeeper's hands, knocked the goalkeeper flying and stuck the ball that remained behind firmly into the net. A foul was blown for this crudely over-enthusiastic piece of play and the following morning Percivall, the headmaster, who happened to have been watching, summoned Arlott and told him he would never play for the school again because of his brutal behaviour.

Blind adolescent rage followed this decision. If he could not play for the school again he was not going to school again. His parents advised him to get his school certificate first and then tell Percivall whatever he wanted, but they were beginning to lose control of their headstrong son, who unilaterally decided he was going to take the school certificate externally. All would have been well there except that, having done enough geography to pass in the first hour of the exam, he left early to go to a cup tie at Reading. The examiner made a note of the fact and he was failed for his arrogance and bad manners. His self-destructive revenge prompted him not to take the exam again. His parents must have suffered much chagrin at his failure to pass school certificate and all that could have entailed, but they did not show it.

There were reasons why their double scholarship boy was leaving school with no qualifications – stubbornness, pride and a refusal to compromise. Yet these same qualities were also behind his greatest successes. His stubborn determination eventually found him a publisher for his anthology of verse and got him out of the police force. Years later, after his retirement, he said he would most like to be remembered for producing Dylan Thomas when he was a literature producer on the Eastern Service of the BBC and for getting Basil D'Oliveira a cricketing job in England. It was pride in his work and refusal to compromise that produced his excellent version of Dylan Thomas's work and the same stubbornness that eventually found D'Oliveira, an unknown coloured cricketer from apartheid South Africa, a job in the Lancashire League after every English county had refused my father's advances on his behalf.

The D'Oliveira connection had started in the late 1950s when my father began to receive polite letters with a South African postmark. Written in green ink, they were from a cricketer he had not met called Basil D'Oliveira. In his autobiography, *Time to Declare*, Basil says that he decided to write to my father because 'his voice and the words he spoke convinced me he was a nice, compassionate man' and that he received 'regular, sympathetic and encouraging letters' back.

Basil wanted to come to England to coach and play professional cricket and had excellent statistics to offer. He had scored eighty centuries in nine years of non-white cricket in South Africa, including 225 in 70 minutes, and once took 9 for 2 with his off-breaks. My father hawked these figures around county club secretaries but they would always say, 'Yes, but on matting wickets against unknown opposition.' My father pointed out that it could not be against known opposition unless they gave him a chance, but nobody was prepared to take that risk.

My father then tried to find Basil a post as a professional in the Lancashire League. The reactions were similar, but in January 1960 a letter arrived from John Kay, a fellow journalist who was closely connected via his brother with the Middleton Cricket Club. Middleton had terminated their contract with the West Indian Roy Gilchrist and had been trying to sign Wes Hall. Wes had been delaying his decision, but late in the day he decided to stay on the right side of the West Indian cricket authorities and turned down the offer. John Kay had remembered my father speaking of Basil D'Oliveira and decided to take a chance. He wrote to my father offering Basil £450 for the season. My father wrote to Basil suggesting he take it, although it was not a huge sum.

At Basil's home in Signal Hill, Cape Town there was great excitement, but how was he to raise the £250 for the fare? His friends took up collections and a white former first-class cricketer, Gerry Innes, also collected £150 for Basil at a whites-only game.

As the day of his departure approached Basil began to get increasingly nervous. What would happen if he could not adapt to the conditions of a cool Lancashire summer and let down all those people who had contributed money? Another white man and former Nottinghamshire county cricketer, Tom Reddick, who had coached in Lancashire, spent the whole of March telling Basil all he knew. It was only when he saw Basil again after he had played for England that he confided that it had been with the greatest difficulty because Basil had been so eager to learn that he had not told him what had been in the back of his mind all the time – stay in South Africa and be a big fish in a small pond. Reddick warned Basil about the poor light and that as the professional in the side he would be a marked man. Inwardly he thought Basil did not have a chance of making it. 'Every stage you passed I thought would be the last one you would be able to master but you kept proving me wrong and made me realise you can always be wrong in this game.'

Tom Reddick would not have been surprised to hear that Basil had made only 25 runs in his first five games and had written to his wife to say he was coming back. Another piece of advice from ex-Lancashire professional Eric Price about the slow, damp early season Lancashire pitches changed everything. 'Wait and relax,' he said. 'The weather will get better and the wickets harder. Until then you've got to wait for the ball to come to you and work it away off the back foot.'

There was someone else who needed to 'wait and relax' – my father, who was phoning Middleton every week for news of his protégé's progress. After the first few depressing weeks there was no need to bother. Basil's scores were so consistently high that he finished his first season top of the averages in the Lancashire League, ahead of Gary Sobers.

My father was doubly delighted. Not only had Basil vindicated his faith in him on a personal level, he also felt that together they had struck a blow against apartheid, a political system that had stopped Basil playing cricket professionally with white men in his own country. My father believed passionately in an individual's right to live in a free society. He and my mother took in German Jewish refugees for years after the war. My father knew of course that several countries were guilty of wicked acts during his lifetime, but he thought that only Nazi Germany and South Africa had actually passed laws that were intrinsically evil.

My father did not have many hatreds, but apartheid and his school headmaster Percivall were two. When he had a hatred he did bear grudges, so when a surprise chance came to avenge himself on Percivall some twenty years later he took it. He attended Queen Mary's Old Boys' dinner every December. The year in question he was telephoned, told that Percivall had asked to attend and invited to make the speech on behalf of his former pupils.

'But surely you remember we hated each other,' said my father, who was beaten more than most by Percivall and still remembered being banned from the school football team.

'We do remember,' said the caller, 'and since most of us

hated him nearly as much as you did we thought you ought to make the speech.'

Having been a campaigning politician by this time in his life as well as a broadcaster, my father was used to speaking in hostile circumstances, so the speech held little terror for him. The dinner passed in a tense atmosphere, and if some of the guests were beginning to feel uneasy the fuse had already been lit.

'Gentlemen, many of you will remember personally the subject of this toast; for them, no description is necessary. For others, the purpose of this speech is simply, with the knowledge of your committee, to recall a single incident in his life.'

My father then described how, to avoid a beating himself, he had hidden behind the coats at the washbasins and watched Percivall beating a frail 12-year-old boy called Woodcock. He added stroke after stroke to the normal three because Woodcock tried to stand up to avoid the blows, and he described how Percivall, who had knocked Woodcock to the ground, turned the boy over with his foot at the end, called him 'a fool' and told him to get up.

'That may remind you, gentlemen, of the headmaster whose health is now proposed – Charles W. Percivall.'

Some applauded overenthusiastically; most remained silent; Percivall left.

In 1929 revenge on Percivall remained a dream, failed school certificate was the reality, my father was 15 and the Great Depression of the 1930s was about to begin.

Work

Through his council contacts my father's father heard of a job as office boy in the planning department. It had none of the drama that starting work can hold. Apart from the lowly nature of the job itself, my father was still living at home and his best schoolfriend, John Carter, was still in town studying for a scholarship.

George Paget, the Planning Officer, was a softly spoken man from Sheffield. He used to send Dad out to get his packets of fifty Rhodesian cigarettes and he was as pleasant an introduction to work as one could want. Unlike the teachers at Saint Mary's school, he was happy to answer my father's thirsting questions. He might have been amused to know that forty-five years later his eager office boy was to lead a crusade in the *Hampshire Magazine* against the destruction of Basingstoke and the 600 per cent increase in its population with London overspill. My father's argument was never against London overspill – he always reminded me that I was London overspill since I was born in Muswell Hill – but that it was necessary to rip the heart out of a perfectly pleasant market town and change its nature when a new town could have been built within Hampshire. Hampshire County Council were so piqued by his constant criticism that an official started one of their monthly meetings by saying, 'John Arlott was not the only person born in Hampshire . . .'

In 1929 my father naively asked, 'So all that green belt you're colouring in around the town will always remain countryside, Mr Paget?'

'Until someone comes along with enough money to change it,' Mr Paget replied prophetically.

After a few months my father saw an advertisement in the *Hants and Berks Gazette* for a diet-clerk at Park Prewett mental hospital for double his then wages – £1 a week. He applied for it and got it. Mr Paget put £1 into his hand and turned away from the thanks, and my father started work in a harder environment. The work was dull but demanding. He had to calculate every morning the amount of food to buy for the patients and staff with as little wastage as possible. Being at the bottom end of the catering staff, he also had to endure the petty office jealousies and cruelties. The threat of the sack was real enough in the 1930s and, given a warning for ordering too much meat on one occasion, he came in even on public holidays to make sure he had got his sums correct.

There was a high percentage of Irish among the doctors because they had the qualifications but not enough money to buy into a practice. They liked hockey, whiskey and chasing the female staff and were genial and approachable. There were many Yorkshiremen among the nursing staff, the new unemployed from the pits and mills who had been prepared to put in enough reading to qualify in another field.

Several of the inmates were intriguing. One who ran the library was learned and seemed totally normal to converse with. My father asked why he had been admitted and was told that if any variation of milk pudding was served he would place his member in it.

It was the time of the Jarrow marches, not a period for casual experimentation in the job market. Dad was still living at home and with his extra ten shillings a week he and John Carter could watch cricket further afield when he could get time off. They also continued to open the innings together for Old St Michael's cricket team. It was four years before he decided on his next step, the police force. His parents did not like the idea of London and he had observed himself that country policemen seemed to work much enforced overtime and to be moved around at whim. A provincial city seemed a good idea, so he wrote off to Bristol, Brighton and Southampton before his annual holiday so that he could get to the interview. Brighton's interview date was after his holiday but both Southampton and Bristol wrote offering employment after the interview. He chose Southampton because he knew it had a strong police force cricket side and allowed him to stay in Hampshire. In those days of unemployment the police could afford to set a height limit of 6ft. My father only just qualified and at six foot and half an inch he was the smallest man on parade in the Southampton force.

Before being allowed to roam the streets as a policeman he had to go to police school at Birmingham, a brutalising experience like most training courses for the uniformed services. Policemen could not be frightened of physical intimidation, so apart from unarmed combat instruction – like judo – there were boxing bouts where the rounds continued until someone got knocked down. The instructors were well able to detect anyone taking a dive and with his love of sport my father was fit enough to get laid out by someone who really knew what he was doing. He had his nose broken failing to avoid a haymaker but used to maintain that it taught him that getting beaten up did not hurt as much as you expected.

As at school his habit of speaking up when others thought it wiser to hold their tongues landed him in the drink with his superiors.

One instructor opened with, 'I don't suppose any of you have seen a dead body.'

'I have,' said my father.

'How many?'

'Four or five hundred,' he exaggerated.

'Where did you work then?'

'A hospital, sir.'

'And how long were you there?'

'Four years, Sergeant.'

'Four or five hundred in four years. I shouldn't have liked to be in your hospital.'

'I am sure you wouldn't, Sergeant. It was a mental hospital.'

This was enjoyed by his fellow trainees but the instructor took his revenge. Until the end of the course he was always 'the one from the loony bin'.

The course bred good friendships because no single personality could have excelled at the office side of police work, life-saving, drill and first aid. Skills were pooled and there was much helping out. My father's skills lay in the written side. Boxing and PT were followed immediately by swimming. When he complained of cramp he was told to stay in the pool to give the life-savers some practice.

The 1930s police haircut was more a scalping and helped the recruits keep together since they were recognised as 'coppers' immediately they stepped out for their two meals a day at Woolworth's cafeteria in the Bull Ring or into a bar on their rare evenings off. Since the trainees came from all over the Midlands and the South the course provided a unique chance for cross-force friendships. The trainees signed each other's obligatory copy of Moriarty's police law at the end, and every policeman had at least one friend of the same age in every police force of the region.

If the trainees from the big cities looked down on those from the countryside or 'soft' towns like Southampton, the old hands from Southampton had some advice for the new police school graduates: 'We don't want any of that Birmingham nick 'em all stuff here. Let people live.'

My father did well enough in the police force, rising to be one of the youngest sergeants the city had had, but police work never really suited him. The average age of the Southampton city force at the time was high. He and one of the few other young policemen in the town, John Creighton, had a reputation for mischief, but it was all fairly harmless for in many ways he was more conventional and obedient than he would have liked to admit. He knuckled under but he never developed that unthinking respect for discipline that uniformed forces attempt to instil. Although he tried to conceal it, he felt a contempt for those in authority who exercised discipline for its own sake.

The most atmospheric but dangerous place for a policeman in a 'safe' town like Southampton was the Below Bar area near the docks, later to be practically wiped out by bombing. In the middle of his evening beat in the early days of his police career a boy ran up to the fresh-faced Arlott (PC 94) and told him breathlessly to come quickly because Tierney (the habitual law breakers were known by name in the Southampton of the 1930s) was holding the 'chippy' over the fat and demanding free fish and chips. Tierney was a drunken, violent Irishman used on local building sites as a kind of human crane because of the amount of heavy material he could move on his back. He seemed distinctly unmoved by the arrival of the stern young police constable. Some months earlier Tierney had despatched an older, heavier police constable through a shop window. My father and other policemen had gone to look at his imprint in the glass, which had been the talk of the force for a few days.

'Put that man down,' my father commanded. The chippy had already fainted through a combination of fear and the heat of the fat – the corners of his white coat were in the chip fat. Tierney and his even more drunken companion were at first disposed to take no notice at all of PC 94, but through the drunken haze they gradually became irritated by his incessant commands to drop the chippy.

'I t'ink de constable wants to go in the chip fat,' Tierney's friend informed him.

With drunken deliberation they dropped the chippy on the floor and moved towards the door where my father was desperately trying to remain calm. Tierney stuck his face in my father's. 'Ach, it's not a real policeman, it's only a boy. Never come to where men are playing again, boy,' he said, pushing Dad so hard backwards into the door that the handle left a bruise on his backside for a month. His colleague followed suit as my father bounced back off the handle. Luckily for my father the boy informant had not much confidence in PC 94's ability to handle the situation and had continued to the police station where he repeated his story. The squad car screeched to a halt and the sergeant leapt towards my father shouting, 'Never, never, never approach Tierney on your own.'

My father later developed a technique for avoiding drunken bar or street fights. He would walk up or enter extremely noisily and slowly so that even the most drunken brawler would inform his mates that a copper was coming and it was time to leave.

PC 94 attended one other celebrated case which kept his name on the lips of his superiors, 'the case of the Bee Hive ring'. The Bee Hive was, and probably still is, a rather nondescript pub on the Millbrook Road. It sported at the time a buxom blonde landlady in her early forties who had in particular one quiet admirer who would ogle her unobtrusively from the corner. Late one winter's night two commercial travellers were at the counter doing their best to shock the unshockable landlady with tales of how large their members were.

'Oh, go on,' she said, 'I've always heard that the quiet ones like Mr Phillips over there are usually the biggest.'

'Not me, Elaine,' said the modest admirer, 'I haven't really got a big one at all.'

'You're just being modest, Mr Phillips.'

'No I'm not, Elaine, it really isn't very big at all.'

'Not so small it could fit into this ring?' she asked, taking a ring off one of her plump fingers.

'Well, it probably could,' said Mr Phillips.

Everyone had been drinking and the landlady was not the retiring sort, so Mr Phillips was finally prevailed upon to place his organ in her ring.

'Well, I never,' she said, giving it a couple of admiring taps, 'it really does fit.' Overcome by her attention, the modest admirer was unable to prevent an erection which was followed by excruciating pain as the ring bit into him and could not be removed. His shouts eventually penetrated the surrounding ribaldry and an ambulance, and for some reason the police, were summoned. Mr Phillips – pain now far outweighing embarrassment – was taken to the Royal South Hampshire Hospital, where the staff were in a quandary over how to treat this first-time case.

The casualty doctor decided that what he really needed was the cutting implement that jewellers use to cut rings off the fingers of fat ladies. My father was despatched to wake up the nearest jeweller and bring him and the implement. Since the jeweller was familiar with the instrument, the casualty doctor prevailed upon him to perform the operation. This successfully achieved, to avoid being woken again at 3 a.m. the jeweller donated the cutters to the casualty department, where they are said still to rest.

Away from such drama my father was still following cricket obsessively. He usually managed to organise his shifts so that he missed few Hampshire games at Southampton. He became a county member and sat in the pavilion only a few feet away from the professionals' balcony. Occasionally someone smiled and said 'good morning'. The county wicketkeeper lived only a few doors away from my father and the fast bowler only a street away. Playing football in Southampton one winter afternoon, my father was surprised to discover that the centre-half marking him was Lofty Herman, the Hampshire fast bowler. They barged one another cheerfully, tripped one another occasionally and met in the local that night.

Holidays were spent watching the cricket with his old schoolfriend from Basingstoke, John Carter, only now they could afford a boarding house and attend matches as far away as Canterbury, Birmingham, Hastings and Brighton.

My father opened the batting for Southampton police when shifts allowed. He was a dull player – back foot, defensive, hard to get out at club level and wearying to spectators and opposition alike. Sometimes he would bowl at the nets at the county ground, making there the deepest and longest of his pre-commentating professional cricket friends, Leo Harrison. Leo was from Mudeford near Christchurch in the southwest of the county. He was on the ground staff and trying to win a place in the county side as a batsman. He was also a wiry, athletic cover point with a whiplash throw. He remembers Dad off – and more often on – duty standing at the back of the nets watching the professionals.

'He was a cricket fanatic but very pleasant. He asked lots of questions and was always at home games, so you just got to know him. I didn't get out of the RAF and back into cricket until 1947 and of course by then I'd heard him on the radio. Could it be the policeman who stood at the back of the nets? I recognised the voice. It must be. I was amazed.'

By 1938 my father was well known to the Hampshire team through his unquenchable support and personable character. When he was watching them on holiday with

John Carter against Kent at Canterbury, Hampshire discovered they would be short of a 12th man for the following day's game against Worcester. A young professional likely to act as 12th man did not have a car in those days, so it was simpler to take someone who could travel with the team. They had no illusions about my father's ability, but they knew that if called upon to field he would put his heart in front of the ball if necessary. Unfortunately it takes more than that, and when an injury put him on the field against Worcestershire a professional square cut whistled past his forehead in the gully before he could move. He was removed to the deep where they knew at least he could run and throw. Being substitute in that one county match was the pinnacle of his playing career.

My father never had any truck with those people who approached him later in a cricket pavilion to confide that their club fast bowler was 'faster than Maurice Tate' or 'faster than Ian Botham'. An amateur player might think Maurice Tate or Ian Botham not very fast compared with some of their professional counterparts, but he would be amazed at just how much quicker they were than the average club fast bowler. If my father ever had any cause to doubt the enormous gulf between club and county professional, an encounter with the Northants professional fast bowler E. W. 'Nobby' Clark that same year fixed itself in his memory. My father was playing for Southampton police and Nobby Clark was playing for a club side for some extra money on the Sunday off in the middle of a county game. He had the prospect of all day in the field on Monday and he had no wish to be still playing club cricket at 7 p.m.

My father opened the batting. Nobby Clark was left-arm fast and unfortunately for Dad moved the ball in to right-handed batsmen. The first ball hit my father on the hip while he was still forming his stroke, rose in a parabola and was caught by the bowler; not that this was witnessed by my father, who was doubled up rubbing his hip bone. The next ball was shorter, hit him in the rib cage and he went down again. In today's less chivalrous climate someone would probably have said, 'Get up or get off', but he was allowed time before the next ball, which missed his stumps by a whisker. He was praying to be bowled, and Nobby must have heard him, for the fourth ball uprooted his leg stump. The other police amateurs fared little better and Nobby got home early to spend some time with his family.

Intimate knowledge of English county professionals after the war may have proved to my father that he could talk about the game more lucidly than most of them, but he never doubted they were in another world when it came to playing.

Marriage

Pre-war Southampton was a pretty law-abiding place and policemen were still regarded as part of the community, so there were no great pressures to prevent my father pursuing his many other ventures. This was just as well as the list of his interests and distractions was long. He was usually in the library reading; charming a succession of landladies into giving a range of benefits normally denied police lodgers; playing and watching cricket and football; socialising and chasing ladies. He also coached badminton, which he played to a good standard – once beating three county players in an afternoon. That also gave him a good chance to meet still more ladies.

The Royal South Hampshire Hospital, which policemen visited frequently in the course of their duty with the injured from drink, fights and accidents, was a favoured happy hunting ground (shop assistants from Boots the Chemists were another favourite target, for reasons I never understood). He had cut a swathe through the girl telephonists at the hospital, who were easily accessible to bored policemen ostensibly waiting for medical reports on victims they had brought in. Thus my mother had seen my father around a fair bit before she accepted a middle-aged Canadian consultant's invitation to go for a spin in his new sports car. He had reached full acceleration down the only

street wide enough for speed in Southampton – the Avenue
through the centre of Southampton Common. The wind
was streaming through my mother's dark hair and the
open sports car was creating just the impression the
consultant had hoped for when a policeman stepped out of
the bushes with his hand raised in an imperious 'Halt'
signal.

'Jesus,' the Canadian said, braking hard, 'it's the police.'
As he screeched to a standstill he recognised the policeman
who was always hovering around the casualty department.

'It's only young Jack Arlott,' he said. Dad looked stern.
He walked slowly round to the passenger side of the sports
car, leant on the door and said, 'Would you like to come
out tonight?' She accepted.

Like most of Dad's *coups de théâtre* there was nothing
spontaneous about it. He had heard the assignation being
made the previous day and had been in the bushes a good
half hour awaiting the roar of an accelerating sports car,
since that was the route they would have to take from the
Royal South Hants into the surrounding countryside.

In fact Southampton Common had already featured in
my mother's life. It was there nearly twenty-five years
before during the First World War that her father, Claude
Rees, a dashing Welsh despatch rider with the 1st Canadian Battalion (he had emigrated to Toronto), charmed
her mother, the daughter of a well-to-do family of south
country butchers, as she served tea to the troops. The
relationship was consummated on the Dover troop train as
he was on his way back to the Somme. When her mother
became pregnant her horrified family insisted on marriage.
It was not a happy one. Claude was the son of a Welsh
builder from Sennybridge in the Brecon Beacons. His
mother died having him, as my father would observe acidly
– there was no love lost between them – and he was sent
off to the naval boarding school of HMS *Mercury* in the
Solent. At the age of 17 he was on the Royal Navy boat

that charted the Great Barrier Reef off Australia's Queensland coast.

He won medals as a dispatch rider on the Somme and was wounded. His wounds cannot have been serious because he lived for another sixty years, but when he died practically penniless in 1981 the Canadian Embassy generously paid for his funeral although he had not been to their country for sixty years.

Claude was musical, a mandolin and banjo player; a good driver at a time when that was a rarer achievement; an excellent golfer and all-round sportsman – 'good at anything that didn't involve work', as Dad would observe charitably. Eventually his brother found him a job selling flour for Rank in Ireland. Claude's version of events was that he made many sales on the golf course and was still owed a large sum of money by Rank when they parted company, a sum he relentlessly pursued in one of his poison-pen letter campaigns afterwards. Dad's version of events was that Claude was unable to sell the flour to the Irish at a time when they were desperate for it because he was too lazy to make the rounds. Certainly my mother has memories of the whole family being activated to flush flour samples down the drains of Wexford, presumably before someone from the organisation called and observed that the house was full of undistributed samples. He was not known for his generosity or for marking family birthdays; he gave my mother a Penguin book for her 21st. He lived in Wexford mainly by selling his wife's heirlooms and furniture, and in later years they communicated by leaving notes for each other in the bathroom.

My mother is a generous and forgiving woman. When she was married to Dad we lived in Highgate, North London. There was a period when my brother and I frequently seemed to be sharing tea with tramps until Dad found a chalk mark on our black gate and rubbed it off.

But my mother had few good words to volunteer for her mother, Madge.

Madge thought Mussolini was wonderful because he made the trains run on time and she used to spend every summer in Italy, leaving Ma and her younger sister and brother to their own devices. Madge's father was the regional director of Dewhurst the butchers. That put my mother – in Madge's eyes at least – a good way above a provincial policeman who was the son of a cemetery keeper. She boycotted my parents' marriage and sent an infamous telegram to the ceremony telling my mother, 'You have married beneath you.' Some things even my mother could not forgive. Madge, who suffered from asthma throughout her life, died in the late 1940s before I was born.

When my grandfather and Rank parted company the family went to live in Wolverhampton, where my mother recalls walking the dog 'crying down to my ankles' because the town was so ugly after the Irish countryside where she had been brought up. It was an escape to begin a nursing career in Southampton.

My father's obsessive reading brought him friends at the public library – Hubert Humby, known as 'Bumble' because he had a permanently preoccupied air, and a red-haired Irishman from Cork named Terry Delaney. Terry spent the last years of the war in Wormwood Scrubs prison in London because of his pacifist views. He refused even to drive an ambulance. After the war my father helped get him into the BBC, where for many years he was a producer on the 'Radio Newsreel' and later the 'World at One' news and current affairs programmes. Terry suspected that his progress further up the BBC ladder was blocked by the habitual BBC board question, 'And what did you do during the war, Mr Delaney?'

He had a pretty wit, exemplified by an incident early in the war when he was returning to Southampton after a day in London. He lived on the Eastleigh side of Southampton, and when the Bournemouth express made an unscheduled stop there Terry got out, blessing his luck at avoiding a three-mile walk home in the cold.

'Oi, you can't get out here,' the guard called to Terry as he slammed the carriage door.

'Why not?' said Terry.

'We don't stop here,' said the guard.

'That's all right,' said Terry, 'I haven't got out.'

Terry's basement flat was scruffily Bohemian, and when he was not lending one of the rooms to various left-wing fringe groups to hold their meetings it was available for friends' courting, which was very useful in those days of strict landladies. It was where my father wooed my mother.

My mother remembers it as being pretty dirty and sparse, but my father took all linen to the Chinese laundry before and after their visits. Shared days off between nursing and police nightshifts were infrequent but the more highly treasured for that. Dad would do the catering, build a strong fire in the grate and make the bed – so he must have been in love.

'He was very tender and sweet,' according to my mother. 'He would read me Oscar Wilde's fairy stories and John Donne poems with an arm around me and assured me he would marry me if anything went wrong. He would treat me like a little girl which I suppose I was really.

'In the morning he would fetch hot rolls from the bakers for breakfast which we would share with much conversation with Terry, and John would buy tins of stew or other convenience food for lunch. It was pretty spartan, I suppose, but it seemed marvellous at the time.'

She found him enormously handsome. He was tall and strong with black wavy hair (he was later to model for the Brylcreem advertisements with Denis Compton) and sharply observant green eyes, and rather a natty dresser. If she was unable to share his love of cricket she did her best to understand. She shared his love of literature, and while cricket was an obsessive hobby literature was his real passion. Despite her upbringing in Ireland my mother speaks with a middle-class English accent because of her English mother. She always lamented that her parents had made no effort with her education other than to send her to the nearest Irish state school, so she was almost as keen as my father to devour the works of famous authors and poets. My father would anyway have bridled at the stereotyped snobbery of thinking there was anything strange about a policeman and a nurse being avid readers of good books and poems.

My father described her as being Celtic in colouring with 'black hair, big blue eyes with almost impossibly splendid lashes, a rosy complexion, full lips and a fine flash of well-made white teeth'. He found she had 'a sense of justice and humour and was a generous, efficient and convivial hostess.'

One day, after my mother and father had been together a good while and had their own flat, they awoke one morning to find the window open wider than it had been and someone under their bed – it was my mother's younger sister Daphne, who had also had enough of Wolverhampton and had run away from home. Claude then began one of his poison-pen crusades, writing to the Chief Constable of Southampton accusing my father of having kidnapped both his daughters. In the police force of those days it was taken seriously enough for Dad to have to appear before the Chief Constable and explain that this was not so. It did not get his relations with his future father-in-law off to a good start, but at least Claude attended the wedding, thus proving that the 'You have married beneath you' telegram was a solitary act by his wife.

While my grandmother was certainly a snob, in class terms for the daughter of a regional sales manager for Rank (albeit a failed one) to marry the son of a country cemetery keeper who was a police constable was of course a step down. In fact it helped my parents' marriage last seventeen years because, while my father had stepped up a social class and become nationally known, my mother only had to cope with the fame. Such enormous changes in fortune often break marriages, but my father had been famous and successful for ten years before their marriage ended.

My parents' courtship had begun just after the outbreak of war. At the time of their marriage in 1940 the 'phoney war' was over and Southampton was being bombed intensively. The city had more air-raid alerts than any other city in Britain. It was a major merchant port with food warehouses at a time when Hitler was trying to starve out Britain. It was also an easy target on a clear night even with the black-out because the town centre and the docks are situated at the bottom of the 'V' made by the rivers Test and Itchen as they enter Southampton Water. Any German bomber that had failed to find its target on a raid of the Midlands and was returning to base without having jettisoned its bombs could make out Southampton.

Southampton got a new Chief Constable at the outbreak of war with instructions to start a War Emergency Department for the city and, on the dubious grounds of his typing ability and a little French, my father was included. Every other night my father had to spend at police headquarters on air-raid duty. To fill in the hours he read – Chesterton, Belloc, Wells, Shaw, Wodehouse, Priestley.

My mother was a nurse at the Royal South Hants at the start of the war and then became night sister at the Children's Hospital. Working nights, my parents were together at home when the first daylight raid came over. They could not resist breaking all instructions and going outside to watch. They saw the celebrated Polish fighter squadron giving the German bombers a frightening introduction to Britain. The Poles were in fact so fanatically anti-Nazi after the fall of Poland that some of them were suspected of suicidally ramming German bombers when they ran out of ammunition. They received a memo from High Command reminding them that Spitfires were too scarce for this course of action no matter what their personal feelings.

Any optimism my parents might have felt was soon dispelled by the night raids. In one of the first raids a huge food store in Southampton docks was hit. The butter burnt for days, killing and injuring several firemen who were trying to put out the blaze, but the worst agony my mother saw in half a lifetime's nursing was when the German bombers hit a tar factory in Totton, covering many of the workers in burning tar.

One night they both returned from night duty within minutes of each other to find their flat had received an indirect hit. The windows were blown in; shards of glass and splinters were embedded in the furniture, but at least most of the contents could be got out and they were happy to be alive. They were evacuated to Chandler's Ford and spent the rest of that winter cycling along often ice-covered roads into Southampton, my father exhorting my mother on as her hands went numb on winter nights and she repeatedly came off the bike onto the icy road.

At the start of yet another raid my father strolled towards the Civic Centre control room as the alert sounded, passing George Brown, the police constable son of the Hampshire and England cricketer of the same name.

'Got to drive the Chief Constable up to Red Lodge,' he said to my father. 'He doesn't like it here when it gets hot.'

'Lucky chap. Enjoy it.'

My father and three policemen on the door dived for cover as a stick of bombs landed nearby. A direct hit on the car killed George Brown. The Chief Constable was still indoors.

After four successive nights of attack with too many buildings burning for the fire service to cope, my father learnt at the Emergency Department that the town would be abandoned if there were another attack. Some police would remain, but the population and hospitals would be moved inland. My father told my mother. When the alert sounded as they were leaving for nightshift they made a tender, frightened farewell, but the German bombers were passing by en route for another target. They did not come to Southampton that night or for the rest of the war.

My father acquired a smattering of Norwegian and German – at least enough to find out the name of a sailor's ship and other basic details – so he was transferred to the Special Branch. Unlike many of his colleagues he obtained his information from official sources, which allowed him to spend an average of two hours a day reading and trying to write poetry in Southampton's pleasant art gallery.

Another unlikely task was debriefing conscientious objectors. My father's friend Terry Delaney was himself a conscientious objector, and Dad had some sympathy with his views.

After my father's death, a Lawrence Thackray wrote to the *Guardian* about being arrested as a conscientious objector in Southampton in 1942:

> I was remanded in custody in Southampton so I could be taken to a medical officer to be examined for military service. A young man in civilian clothes visited me, and we engaged in a long discussion on conscientious objection – why I held these views, what had influenced me, my reading. The young man was courteous, shrewd, fair. The conversation ranged widely – it seemed to go on for an hour or two. Somehow at one stage it centred on Elizabethan poetry and this unusual police officer (for so I assumed he was) informed me modestly that he was trying to produce an anthology of poetry of that period.
>
> He took me to my medical which, not to his surprise,

I refused. Back in my cell he gave me a parting gift of *The Good Soldier Schweik* and 20 Weights (cigarettes).

Many years later I saw such an anthology in a bookshop and realised that my interrogator had been John Arlott.

One way my father got to know several established authors was by sending them his copy of their books to sign. He would include a carefully thought out letter saying what he had liked about their books. This was easy to do because he only sent them to authors he genuinely admired. It was probably why he fastidiously replied to all letters he received when he became well known – because he remembered the disappointment of receiving nothing back when he was just a provincial policeman. He was not thick-skinned. He was also polite enough to be aware of the possibility of wasting busy people's time, so I was quite surprised to learn that as a young man he had made a habit of writing to famous authors he did not know, but he was driven by ambition, self-confidence and his collector's zeal. While he was particularly happy to get a friendly reply from the author himself, he was also quite content just to have the books signed for his collection.

My father was interested in topography and greatly appreciated John Betjeman's Shell Guides to Devon and Cornwall, and his verse collections *Mount Zion, Continual Dew* and *Old Lights for New Chancels*. Betjeman was then far from a household name and my father wrote to him asking if he would collaborate on a book of topographical poetry. He wrote back encouragingly but saying he was already committed to an anthology of landscape poetry with Geoffrey Taylor. Undeterred, my father wrote to Oxford University Press suggesting a collection to be called the 'Oxford Book of Topographical Poetry' with a list of well-known and not so well-known poems he had found in his researches covering every English county. Oxford University Press rejected the idea, but the literary critic George Rostrevor Hamilton agreed to collaborate and sent the idea to Cambridge University Press where it was accepted by Sydney Roberts.

My father joyfully started work. The anthology consisted of celebrated poems about English counties, but when he wrote to the then poet laureate John Masefield asking for permission and terms for using a poem of his about Worcestershire, Masefield's agent wrote back saying, 'Please do not address Mr Masefield directly again.' My father asked George Rostrevor Hamilton if he might attempt to write one himself. He called it 'Cricket at Worcester 1938':

> Dozing in deck chair's gentle curve
> Through half closed eyes I watched the cricket
> Knowing the sporting press would say
> 'Perks bowled well on a perfect wicket.'
>
> Fierce mid-day sun upon the ground,
> Through heat haze came the hollow sound
> Of wary bat and ball, to pound
> The devil from it, quell its bound.
>
> Sunburned fieldsman, flanelled cream
> Seemed, though urgent, scarce alive,
> Swooped like swallows of a dream
> On skimming fly, the hard hit drive.
>
> Beyond the score box, through the trees
> Gleamed Severn, blue and wide,
> Where oarsmen feathered with polished ease
> And passed in gentle glide.
>
> The back cloth setting off the setting
> Peter's Cathedral soared
> Rich in shade and fine of fretting
> Like cut and painted board.

To the Cathedral, close for shelter
Huddled houses, bent and slim,
Some tall, some short, all helter skelter
Like a sky-line drawn for Grimm.

This the fanciful engraver might
In his creative dream have seen,
Here, framed by summer's glaring light,
Grey stone, majestic over green.

Closer the bowler's arm swept down
The ball swung, pitched and darted
Stump and bail flashed and flew;
The batsman pensively departed.

Like rattle of dry seeds in pods,
The warm crowd faintly clapped,
The boys who came to watch their Gods,
The tired old men who napped.

The members sat in their strong deck-chairs
And sometimes glanced at the play,
They smoked and talked of stocks and shares,
And the bar stayed open all day.

George Rostrevor Hamilton corrected a few errors and included it in the anthology. Unbidden, he also sent it to Cyril Connolly, the editor of *Horizon*. My father received a letter of acceptance out of the blue from Connolly and, enormously encouraged, he sent off other poems to the *Observer* and the *Fortnightly Review* which were also accepted. A long time later he had the chance to ask Connolly why he had accepted 'Cricket at Worcester'.

'I hate cricket,' Connolly said, 'but when I was a boy my uncle used to take me to watch county matches and it was exactly as in your poem.'

In 1943 my parents moved into a house in Lodge Road, Southampton and my father took out an option to buy. My father's parents gave him some furniture and they drove up and down to Basingstoke in borrowed vans to fetch it. One possible bone of contention with the neighbours was the garden, in which my father had no interest. Happily his father also took care of that when he came to stay.

My father already knew Lodge Road from visits to Sam and Doris 'Mingo' Saunders, who became life-long friends. Sam was a GP in Southampton for nearly forty years, but he and his wife were bombed out of their house in Lodge Road before my parents moved.

Unlike Leo Harrison, 'Mingo' was not the least surprised that the police constable who had come round selling them tickets for the police ball and stayed to tea later became a household name.

'I knew from the beginning he wouldn't remain a copper. He wasn't very interested in the police force. He was madly keen on reading, interested and intelligent. Even when he was on traffic duty he would try to read at the same time. He was huge company and a delight to entertain.'

In December 1943 the most exciting event of my father's life so far occurred. *Landmarks*, an anthology of topographical poems selected by George Rostrevor Hamilton and John Arlott, was published. Soon afterwards my mother became pregnant and gave up night duty. There were occasional flying bomb attacks, but in comparison with the early days of the war my parents were safe and, on 4 December 1944, James Andrew John Arlott – Jim – was born.

The Climb

How did a provincial policeman become a BBC cricket commentator at a time when a public school accent was obligatory to get on the air? My father used to answer this question by saying it was 'a series of flukes'. Luck was involved and the good fortune of having remained in Britain at a time when many more obvious candidates were fighting overseas. I was so used to him referring to 'flukes' and 'luck' that I was startled one night when we were having dinner alone in the National Liberal Club shortly before his retirement to be contradicted when I repeated such descriptions of his rise to success.

'If I hadn't made it that way I would have made it some other way,' he replied. He was right. At that period of his life he was beating on so many doors at the same time it was just a question of which one gave way first. He was pouring information into his brain – poetry, literature and anything else that was opportune or caught his fancy. Often in that period he would sit on the toilet until 5 a.m. finishing his second book of the day in an unsuccessful attempt to avoid keeping my mother awake.

What helped him more than the fact that an amazing amount of the knowledge being poured in was being retained, was that he had an agreeable and interesting personality. People liked him. He had enthusiasm and drive and most people were willing to help – like John Parker, the head of Southampton University's Extramural Department, whom my father met in a pub. John Parker offered my father the University library to research his current craze of modern Russian history and military strategy. Later, content that my father was both articulate and had become an instant expert, he offered him the chance to give lectures on Russian history and military strategy to units of the armed forces stationed in the area – and there were plenty of units around Southampton and the south kicking their heels as they waited for D-Day. These lectures were to prove a useful training ground for commentaries because servicemen demanded something stimulating if their interest was to be held. John Parker had already told my father the cautionary tale of John Gielgud's recitation of Shakespearean monologues to the submariners stationed near Portsmouth.

Fearing a low turnout, the submariners' commanding officer made attendance compulsory. The legendary actor began with 'To be or not to be'. 'Give us a song,' said the perennial voice from the back. Gielgud dramatically recomposed himself: 'To be or not to be, that is the question.'

'Give us a song,' pursued the submariner.

'I know,' said Gielgud, 'that some of you have not had the chance – and perhaps think you might not want the chance – to hear Shakespeare's finest monologues, but I assure you that if you give me a chance you will see that they still have something to tell everybody.' Pause.

'To be or not to be, that is the question
Whether 'tis nobler in the mind to suffer
The slings and arrows of outrageous fortune . . .'

'If you're not going to give us a song, show us your cock,' the voice suggested.

My father hoped his lectures would have more immediate popular appeal.

On his two days off a week an army lorry would take

him to the base where he was scheduled to give a talk. If the talks did not seem to be furthering a career, the £10 extra a week certainly helped.

At the University library he made two new friends – Reg Loader, a lecturer in Classics, and Harry Howell, a physicist. Loader, a Geordie who wrote an excellent book about running called *Staying the Distance*, was kept out of the war by his poor eyesight but eventually his classical Greek 'won' him a place as a radio operator on a Greek tanker. Howell had already demonstrated how a ray could stop an internal combustion engine. He freely admitted that the ray could not do it if a fireguard was put in front of the engine, but officialdom continued to pay for his research in the hope he would produce a more warlike scientific breakthrough.

Howell loved Damon Runyon. Runyon's present tense, understated gangster yarns lent themselves to being read aloud and Harry Howell would make my parents laugh. 'I am sitting in Mindy's eating gefilte fish when who should come in but Harry the Horse. I am not too pleased to see Harry the Horse but I would not let on to this for much money.'

As my mother mused afterwards, she was still learning to cook and they had little enough to offer the stream of academic friends from George Rostrevor Hamilton to John Betjeman who came to the house, so my father must have had something. He was as good a listener as talker. He had a grand sense of humour and was interested in everybody and everything connected with literature, education and sport.

Because of his forces' lectures and the few poems he had had published, he was recruited to join the ENSA Brains Trust gathered to entertain the forces. This provided more handy pocket money and another new friend in Michael Ayrton, son of the poet Gerald Gould and Barbara Ayrton

Gould, who was Chairman of the Labour party for a while. Michael became a well-known artist.

My father was still trying to write poetry, endlessly polishing and repolishing the finished product with which he was never satisfied. As well as John Betjeman, he greatly admired Andrew Young, a parson poet, who wrote mainly about nature and the countryside. He sent Young a poem in praise of his work which was later published. He got to know him and Young officiated at my brother Robert's christening when he was an old man some twenty years later. Upright, unbent by age even in his eighties, he was a rather taciturn Scot. My brother, stepmother and I chose the last two lines of the poem for the headstone of my father's grave.

TO ANDREW YOUNG
On reading his poems

> Behind these limpid words I find
> Reflections in a crystal mind,
> Of images so sharp and clear
> That I can almost see and hear
> The subjects of your calm delight.
> The spider-webs of which you write
> Are not more accurate, more fine,
> More integral, more light of line,
> Nor spun by wisdom more innate
> Than are these lines where you create
> With living eye, with living hand,
> Your real and visionary land:
> So clear you see these timeless things
> That, like a bird the vision sings.

My father's real break came out of the blue. John Betjeman mentioned to a BBC Talks producer, Geoffrey Grigson, that he had come across a policeman who was addicted to poetry. Grigson wrote to my father asking if he would give a radio talk on being a policeman who liked poetry. He nearly blew his chance by replying that he was not prepared to be regarded as a freak but would be happy to do a broadcast. Grigson replied that if he destroyed his own news value he would need to be a good broadcaster but, probably because there was little enough young male talent around during the war, he asked my father to Bristol for an audition.

Perhaps he also had in mind to show the rather cocksure young policeman that broadcasting was not easy. He gave him an extract from Coleridge's *Biographia Literaria* to read. It ran nearly two and a half pages without any meaningful punctuation. My father studied it carefully for several minutes and read it with as much meaning as he could.

Grigson said, 'That was all right.'

Years later my father discovered that Grigson had written in his report, 'This man is a natural broadcaster and should be encouraged.'

'Now we have to find out if you can write,' said Grigson. 'What we want is a kind of lay sermon for one of those Sunday night postscripts.'

Back at Lodge Road my father laboured over one radio talk script after another, but his lack of scriptwriting experience showed and Grigson rejected them all. In desperation he turned to his love of cricket and wrote a piece called 'The Hampshire Giants', about the eighteenth-century Hambledon village cricket club captained by Nyren that defeated the All England XI thirty-seven times between 1772 and 1796. It was a startlingly good piece of radio journalism for someone without experience. Maybe the experience of forces lectures helped him hold the interest of the ordinary listener. He was asked to broadcast it and the *Listener* magazine printed it in full in 1945.

Listening tensely to that first pre-recorded broadcast was the first time my father had ever heard himself speak in those days before tape recorders became a common household possession. His Hampshire accent was so strong to his ear that he could not believe it was him.

He was desperately disappointed. 'They've got some country chap in to read it,' he said forlornly to my mother after the first few sentences.

'Don't be silly,' she laughed. 'It's you.'

In fact my father was not at all pleased to hear the strength of his country accent. He sensed, probably correctly, that it would hold him back in the Oxbridge-dominated BBC of the 1940s. He even set about trying to eradicate it at one stage until a broadcasting colleague, Valentine Dyall, said he would 'rip his tongue out' if he continued to do something so stupid and unnatural.

Events were beginning to overtake him. As he was fretting over how he could get the days off to do another broadcast, the BBC producer Jack Dillon asked him if he would like to compere 'Country Magazine'. He found it difficult to answer without shouting for joy, but the war was ending and strangely his next broadcast was to be on behalf of the police force. Together with the armed services, the police had been asked to make an address to the King on Victory Night. The BBC asked for my father because he had broadcast before and the police compromised – your man, our script. The script read like a police graduation day speech but, egged on by the BBC producer, who assured him no one would notice, my father rewrote it and predictably there were no complaints.

Southampton Police Training School had been using my father as a lecturer on Aliens, Special Branch and Wartime Emergency Legislation. Just before the end of the war he was removed from this thrilling topic and sent to Peel House in London where the Metropolitan Police were setting up a new police instructors' training school. While he was in London, the *Radio Times* journalist Campbell Nairn came to write a background piece on the constable who had spoken the police tribute in the address to the

King. They got on well and Nairn asked him if he had seen the BBC job vacancy for an Overseas Literary Producer. My father said surely he would not be considered for such a post, but Nairn replied, 'You never know.'

My father searched for the advertisement everywhere but it was not until the day he was returning to Southampton that he found it in the *Listener* on Waterloo station.

In Southampton he was back on constable duties though promoted to Acting Sergeant, but he was becoming increasingly aware that away from London he was 'out of sight and out of mind'. The only chance was the job application. A reply came giving the date and time for an interview but it was the day of the annual police parade. He went straight to see the Chief Constable, who was far less disciplinarian than his predecessors, told him about the interview and mournfully pointed out that it coincided with the government inspection.

'What difference does that make?' asked the Chief Constable.

'Well, Sir, the government inspector asks for the youngest sergeant to drill the parade and I am not very good at drill.'

'I know that, Sergeant, so you will no doubt find an important enquiry to make at Portswood.'

My father planned the interview meticulously, borrowing Michael Ayrton's flat which was close to the BBC. He took a cold bath and dressed with care. My father was a natural pessimist, so he kept himself calm by thinking of the thousands of young writers returning all the time from the war who might have seen the advertisement and how he must not delude himself into thinking his chances were anything but minimal.

He stayed calm and the interview seemed to go well enough. The reaction that greeted the acceptance letter on the doormat was a different matter. Immediately panicky fears arose about the red tape of police service, the details of which he knew only too well. Once more he stammered out a demand for an appointment with the Chief Constable and burst in on him.

'Congratulations, Arlott, when do you go?'

'But, Sir, the Home Office instructions say a policeman can only leave the force if he is over the years of service or sick.'

'Well, you are sick, Arlott, aren't you?'

And the hysterically risky reply, 'I'm sick of police duty, Sir.'

'That has been apparent to me for a long time, Arlott. You'd better go.'

Profuse thanks were followed by celebrations. On the first morning after his final day of police duty he put the alarm clock on for 'early turn'. When it rang he threw it out of the window. He would never walk those long beats around Southampton Common again.

London

'One crowded hour of glorious life is worth an age without a name' – not one of my father's favourite quotations though he would have happily ventured 'Thomas Mordaunt, 1791' between mouthfuls of lunch if you had quoted it at him. This postwar period was full of 'crowded hours' as unexpected chances piled on top of each other.

When he landed the job of Overseas Literary Producer at the BBC and had to move immediately to London, it was my father's friend from the ENSA Armed Forces brains trust, Michael Ayrton, and his partner Joan who had him to stay with them in their two-floor flat at the back of All Souls Place, the cul-de-sac between Broadcasting House and All Souls Church. The other occupants were the ballerina Margot Fonteyn, whom both my parents liked, and the composer, conductor and pianist Constant Lambert.

Although my father was already over 30 when he went to London, the dawning thrill of having landed the BBC producer's job and the stimulating, intelligent company lent London the same excitement it would have had to a provincial teenager seeing it for the first time.

His arrival coincided with the first Promenade Concerts season after the war and Constant Lambert was appearing frequently. Despite several drinks with my father and

Michael in 'The George', he never went to bed without practising and would run through a series of test pieces. One was particularly difficult, and if he made an error he would return determinedly to the beginning. The whole household would wait tensely in their beds until he finished the piece. He would then play anything less taxing that took his fancy and turn in.

The BBC Overseas Literary Producer's office was at 200 Oxford Street. My father shared a room with Sunday Wilshin, an actress who had once understudied for Gertrude Lawrence and was not interested in men, and their two secretaries. He had to produce three programmes, two of them weekly. The most stimulating and enjoyable consisted of a half hour of criticism and quotations from a poet or group of poets. He could choose the critics, readers and poets. There was also a fifteen-minute programme with the same format but with only one reader and critic.

My father was passionately fond of poetry. To be able to choose which poets he would broadcast, handpick readers who shared his enthusiasm and get paid for it was a heady freedom after the constraints of police work. One poet who to his delight was always happy to claim the broadcast fee involved was Dylan Thomas, whose work he had long admired from a distance. To heighten the pleasure he found Dylan more than willing to have a drink after the programme, and grand company. Dylan took to going to the 'Old Mother Red Cap' public house in Camden Town on Saturday mornings with my father because he enjoyed the absurd imagination of one of the undertakers who used the pub at that hour. The undertaker would tell Dylan about coffin lids that would not fit on because the corpse had an enormous erection, and, flattered by his receptive audience, he would try to have a new offering for them each week. Needless to say, he had no idea who Dylan was and would not have cared if he had.

Another time Dylan took to buying a weekly American

magazine and retiring to a table to study the contents minutely before rejoining the group at the counter. One of the magazine's lady reporters had been sent over to Britain to do 'in depth' research on Dylan and had taken her instructions literally. After a month or so the long awaited issue arrived. The article was large and easy to find.

'Blubber-lipped, gooseberry-eyed Welsh poet Thomas,' Dylan read dejectedly to his companions. 'Bloody hell, and she said she loved me.'

My father defended Dylan against stories of continual drunkenness, pointing out that he took his work too seriously to drink while writing and that he spent a lot of his time writing, but he did once watch him hand a pint glass to the barman and tell him to empty a short from each bottle on the top shelf into it. Such behaviour smacks of 'the insult to the brain' that an American coroner was later to say was the cause of his death.

Dylan was a component of my father's second regional love – South Wales. Long after my father had given up the Literary Producer's job for cricket commentary, Dylan would come to the ground if it was a Glamorgan game, curl up in the back of the commentary box, and later take Dad to the many Swansea haunts where he was liked and known.

Dylan did most of his radio broadcasts for my father. Most poets cannot read their own or anybody else's work to professional standard because it is only an arbitrarily related skill, but Dylan could and he took his acting seriously. He would accept direction, and his style of reading at a continual near-climactic pitch is instantly recognisable.

There was a mutual fan club element to their friendship, with Dylan writing to Dad once from Tuscany: 'It was good to hear from you. Though I hear your voice every day: from Trent Bridge at the moment. You're not only the best cricket commentator – far and away that; but the best sports commentator I've heard, ever; exact, enthusiastic, prejudiced, amazingly visual, authoritative, and friendly. A great pleasure to listen to you: I do look forward to it.'

When Dylan died, my father burnt any letters which might not have shown him in a good light.

George Orwell had been the BBC Overseas Literary Producer before my father and he left notes for him on most of the regular contributors. He advised against trying to produce the novelist E. M. Forster, who was giving the monthly book talk to India. Forster did not use simple English. He thought the listener should make the effort to meet the broadcaster halfway and that broadcasts should be intellectually stimulating. Once he arrived in a thick muffler fixed with a large safety pin which my father was convinced must be making him uncomfortably hot in the studio. He asked him if he wanted to take it off, but Forster said his mother had put it on and he was sure he would not be able to put it back properly. However, he was not a soft man. When my father suggested he might like to tone down criticism of a fellow author my father liked, Forster replied, 'That is what I think about him and that is what I should like to say about him.'

One day he wrote in polite but certain terms to say he did not wish to continue his monthly broadcast. My father did not see him for many years until one day he was asked to tea for no reason he could think of. Eventually Forster volunteered that he had heard my father on an 'Any Questions' programme attacking discrimination against homosexuals.

'I thought it was courageous, what you had to say about homosexuality,' Forster said.

That was kind, my father replied, but it had been easily done because it was what he believed.

'One thing you didn't say, though,' Forster added.

'What was that?' said my father.

'It's such fun.'

My father employed scriptwriters for the 'Book of Verse' and his other programmes as well as readers. His favourite scriptwriter was a large, balding, relaxed, amusing Dubliner called Harry Craig. At one period he came to lunch every Sunday. Harry was usually late for lunch, once assuaging my father's anger by informing him he had managed to chat up a foreign girl who spoke no English on the tube, consummating the relationship on the back stairs of Russell Square station. Ascending an escalator with my father on another occasion and regarding the perfumed, coiffured office girls descending a few feet away, he lamented, 'Does it never worry you, John – the number of them you'll never have?'

He was a talented man for whom fame came too late in life when his two film scripts on the Crimean War were produced.

Robin Holmes, who read the BBC Radio News for twenty years, made his debut on my father's programme, as did David Jacobs. Both remained warm and thankful whenever he came across them in their later careers. They both had light, clear, responsive voices. For variety my father used the actor Valentine Dyall, who had a startlingly deep voice and was already well known to radio listeners of the time as 'the Man in Black'. For more emotional items he turned to Celts like Duncan MacIntyre or Dylan Thomas.

My father still had much to learn about broadcasting. He would joke afterwards that he had the luck to make all his mistakes on the Indians and other overseas listeners who dare not complain for fear the service would be stopped. In fact his passion and commitment to make a success of those early programmes shone through. Recordings show them to be totally different from the dated, Oxbridge-accented programmes of the time. He was proudest of his production of Dylan Thomas's writing, but Duncan MacIntyre's 'Bonny Earl of Murray' is highly moving and he and my father worked for hours on the poem 'Timor Mortis Conturbat Me'. Those words end every verse and Duncan MacIntyre utters them with a different pitch and emotion each time to match the content of the verse. The finished product shows that the effort was worthwhile.

Not all was success. There was one early attempt to make a distinguished literary contact that backfired. My father had long admired Norman Douglas, the author of *South Wind*. He had a reputation as a difficult man with unusual sexual inclinations, but my father decided to ask him to dinner although he had never met him. He and Michael Ayrton had decided that surely no man could resist an invitation to dine at the Savoy, even from a stranger.

Douglas wrote a terse letter of acceptance, and a fortnight later my father and Michael were awaiting his arrival in the Savoy in their best suits. Douglas was late and eventually they decided to wait for him at the table, leaving word with the head waiter. When Douglas arrived, he walked assuredly to their table, sat down without introduction, beckoned the waiter, took the menu and ordered at high speed. Dad and Michael followed on lamely with their own orders. Douglas made no effort at all to reply to their small talk and attacked his lobster bisque as soon as it struck the table. To most enquiries he did not bother to grunt a reply, and as Dad and Michael could see that further interrogation was futile the pause between courses passed slowly and tensely.

Douglas held up his glass to be refilled at regular intervals and finally went a course ahead of them. My father and Michael had got quite used to talking between themselves as their guest accepted his cognac, drained it in one, pushed back his chair, stood up, wiped his face with his napkin and announced, 'Cats are no good, not even greased and wedged in a jackboot.'

He left. Dad and Michael were unanimous that this advice was not worth a four-course meal in the Savoy, but after a cognac my father decided to add insult to injury by buying two bottles of Tokay Essence, the famed dessert wine of the Hungarian Emperors which was on the wine list at thirty shillings. It seemed the reckless end to a ridiculous evening, but when he read some twenty years later that a bottle of Tokay had gone for £80 at a wine auction my father decided the undrunk second bottle would choke him at that price and put it up for auction, getting back, by his calculations, the whole meal at the Savoy including inflation.

My father was so delighted to be able to indulge his love of literature professionally that winter that his cricket obsession had never been further from his thoughts. Both he and my mother confirmed that he would have been perfectly happy, if less well known, to have remained a producer of literary programmes all his life. The lucky break as far as my father was concerned was from the police force to being a producer at the BBC, not from literary producer to cricket commentator.

Donald Stevenson, Head of the BBC Overseas Service, volunteered at a programme meeting that he had heard that the Indian cricket team would be touring England the coming summer.

'We must show them that we know the side has come. When do they start to play?'

'The first Saturday in May,' my father replied.

'Ah yes,' said Stevenson, 'I remember from your job interview you are keen on cricket. We could get a feed from domestic services – they will certainly be covering it . . . no, damn it, they would get the Indian pronunciations wrong. Have you ever done a cricket broadcast?'

'Yes,' said my father, stretching the truth but thinking of his broadcast on the 'Hampshire Giants'.

It was resolved that if my father could do the cricket broadcasts without interfering with his poetry programmes he would do the opening matches against Worcestershire and Oxford University to show the Indians that the BBC World Service knew there was an Indian touring team in the country. With no thought to days off with the family, as ever, he grabbed the chance.

While trying to appear blasé at this thrilling offer my father also had to find a house for my mother and Jim. Michael Ayrton's flat had given a taste for central London, but the sale of a lease on a house in Lodge Road, Southampton – even with the better BBC salary – was never going to allow a free choice of London suburbs, so a terraced house in Barrington Road, Crouch End was all they could afford. (Coincidentally, Barrington was to be the surname of my mother's second husband after my parents' divorce.) They moved in during the winter of 1945.

They were rarely alone as a family in Barrington Road. First, my parents put up a homeless German Jew, Dieter Weil, a stonemason who had managed to get out of Germany in time and spent the war in the Pioneer Corps. Now the war was over he had no relatives in Britain, nowhere to live and no job, though he later found work in a condom factory. He stayed for eighteen months and eventually emigrated to Australia. Karl Marx's niece, who was a nurse, was another homeless German Jew who stayed for a while.

Spring 1946 brought the challenge of my father's first cricket broadcasts. The Indian captain, the Nawab of Pataudi, who played for Worcestershire, pretended to remember the young man who had fielded 12th man for Hampshire at Worcester before the war, and the Indian side were pleased that their opening games were to be broadcast to India.

The broadcasts only lasted a few minutes, and my

father's main difficulty was knowing when to switch from the summary of the day's play to the action in front of him. The cricket broadcaster's fear is being in the middle of reading a written summary, notes or the scorecard at the instant when the listener can hear an explosion of unexplained 'live' applause for a four or the fall of a wicket. However, by the end of the Oxford University match he thought he was getting better at keeping one eye on the details and one eye on the play.

The experience approached bliss when on the second day of the Oxford game he was sitting in a bomb crater at the edge of the Parks watching the play with Dylan Thomas, Louis MacNeice and Cecil Day Lewis. His passions were fused. It was mesmerising to think that someone was paying him to sit in this company watching a game he loved.

When he returned to 200 Oxford Street the next day, he found a message asking him to see Donald Stevenson. He mounted the stairs, his head full of possible complaints. Stevenson tossed him a cable from Jim Pennethorne-Hughes, the BBC's Delhi correspondent: 'Cricket broadcasts greatest success yet East Service. Must be continued at all costs, Hughes.'

Stevenson asked my father if he wanted to continue to the end of the season, but warned him that there must be no falling off in the quality of his literature programmes. The cricket was strictly a sideline.

Now he was to get to tour England watching cricket. He had been around Hampshire; to Eastbourne and back on a bicycle; he now lived in London; and had been to police school and cricket at Birmingham. But he had never been north of the Trent nor had time to get to know those attractive grounds and places where county cricket is played, like Bath, Cheltenham, Scarborough, Cambridge, Ebbw Vale – where the seats are carved out of the chalk in the hillside – and by Mumbles Bay at Swansea.

His tour around England with cricket sides was to become a procession from one group of friends to another. His position as a commentator gave him *carte blanche* to enter county dressing rooms and talk to players whose careers until then he had only followed in the newspapers. He loved the company of professional cricketers, whom he found modest, friendly and intelligent. I heard him ruminate many times that it is the nature of the game, with its unparalleled, sudden and final difference between success and failure, that seems to make those who play it more human and individual than other sportsmen. The way, for instance, that character shines through an innings – whether it is constructed with the extrovert attacking genius of a Keith Miller or an Ian Botham or the steely concentration of a Geoff Boycott or a Bill Lawry.

Keeping up with his literary programmes often meant getting the sleeper from Manchester or Leeds, tube and bus to Crouch End and breakfast, into Oxford Street to record 'Book of Verse' and the prose programme, a couple of drinks with the production team, and the night sleeper back to Manchester. But it was all exhilarating.

My mother's first dinner for cricketers when the Indian touring side were playing at Lord's had the makings of disaster. My father had invited Merchant, Hazare and Mankad. He had told my mother they would not eat meat but had not known that they would not eat fish or eggs either and of course strictly no alcohol. Fortunately there was enough rice and potatoes in the house and the guests cheerfully waved aside apologies.

The BBC 'staff no fee' idea was popular with programme planners, so towards the end of the season the BBC regions asked my father to do commentaries on the counties for the home audience if there was no regular commentator present. Daydream offers were becoming commonplace; it was a landmark he took in his stride.

At the end of the season the Head of BBC Outside Broadcasts, S. J. Lotbiniere, sent for my father.

'While I think you have a vulgar voice you have a compensatingly interesting mind. Would you like to broadcast on next summer's South African tour?'

The manner of asking revealed a snobbery my father was to come across again in that period, but there was only one possible answer to the question. He greatly enjoyed his literature programmes and was given permission to continue with them as well.

While still in Southampton my father had been fascinated by the Roman landing site on Southampton Water. He and Michael Ayrton had decided to produce a book of sonnets and lithographs of the site and to their partners' derision once spent the night there under waterproof sheets to help get a feel for the place. The book that resulted, *Clausentum*, came out in 1946 and almost at once the publishers Longmans asked him to write his first book of prose on the previous summer's Indian tour. Like all requests at the time it was accepted, although it meant starting work after dinner and continuing into the small hours. He bashed out the whole 60,000-word book, in his violently fast but inaccurate three-fingered typing style, in ten nights. It was called *Gone to the Cricket* and was to be the start of a habit – writing books about the previous summer's tour in the winter nights that followed.

The following year my father's boss Donald Stevenson was promoted and Jim Pennethorne-Hughes returned from Delhi to take over. He and my father became instant friends. The summer of 1947 was the Compton–Edrich year when the sun seemed to shine every day and the Middlesex and England pair broke every scoring record and made all opponents, including the South African tourists, suffer. My father was beginning to master the commentary trade. When the South African left-arm spinner 'Tufty' Mann had the Middlesex and England batsman George

Mann in all sorts of difficulties, Dad pronounced the first of many oft quoted 'one liners'. It was, he said, 'a case of man's inhumanity to man'.

The intimate knowledge of touring teams picked up by travelling with them also provided insights into the difficulty of the game at Test level. South Africa lost the series 3-0, but in their valiant attempt to win the last Test at the Oval and salvage some pride their opener Bruce Mitchell scored a century in both innings. Mitchell battled throughout the second innings and 'Tufty' Mann told my father afterwards that he had been taken aback after he had been batting for half an hour when Mitchell struck a four and they met in the middle of the pitch. Mitchell looked him in the face and said surprised, 'Tufty? But where's George?' George Fullerton had been out more than half an hour before, but such was Mitchell's concentration that he had never noticed the fall of Fullerton's wicket or that he had been batting with a new batsman for the last half hour.

The books continued: an account of the summer's South African tour in the winter and an anthology of British poems that had never been published in the United States, called *First Time in America*. Dylan Thomas was asked to contribute and produced two poems for this anthology. Meanwhile the eccentricity of the BBC continued to surprise. One day a lady from the religious department phoned to ask if he could write hymns. 'I expect so,' said Dad, 'but I've never tried.' He omitted to mention that he was a convinced atheist. She wanted three; when did he think they might be ready?

'Tomorrow,' Dad replied. The lady took umbrage, so – never one to duck a challenge – my father worked into the night and had three hymns on the Harvest Festival, Rogation and Plough Sunday on her desk the following morning. All three were published in the BBC Hymn Book and have provided a steady trickle of royalties ever since.

The hymn on the Harvest Festival was set to the English traditional melody 'Shipston', which was just as well as my father could no more have fitted the music than designed a spacecraft. Music was one of his blind spots. My mother, who loves music, encouraged my brother Jim with his singing and used to take me to listen to him when he became a boy chorister with Hampstead Parish Church. Jim sang on record with the choir and made a tour of Sweden with them. My father was proud of my brother's musical ability. But I do not remember him ever going to church to listen to him, though he enjoyed it when my brother was older, played the guitar and sang folk songs. My mother once asked my father how a man who professed to love the arts could have no feeling for music. 'I do like music,' he said, 'but there is so much to learn that I could never get to the bottom of it.'

Dad was driven to swallow every fact and respected book on passions like literature, topography, wine and cricket. If it was going to be too difficult to have an encyclopaedic knowledge of a subject, then it was not worth starting. He had an extreme, uncompromising mind.

As for my father's hymns, those on Rogation and Plough Sunday sunk into relative obscurity but the Harvest Festival hymn is sung frequently and not only in England. We were about to sit down to dinner twenty years later when a clergyman phoned from America to ask if he could change the word 'reaping', which he claimed his American congregation did not understand. My father, who hated having his work tampered with, shouted charitably to me from the dining room that the clergyman could change it to what he liked if he sent a cheque for $5,000. The clergyman might well have decided that, since he was 5,000 miles away, he would change it to whatever he liked, but since he was honest and diligent enough to find our phone number and call, he probably did not.

My father found the 1948 Test series highly stimulating. If English supporters were quietly confident after the record-breaking Edrich–Compton summer that their team would beat 'the old enemy', they were sadly mistaken.

Many cricket experts have argued that the 1948 Australians were the strongest Test side ever assembled. Defeat never seems to deter English cricket supporters, who turned up in ever larger numbers to see their side humiliated. They lost the series 4-0 and, while that figure has been matched, the 1948 Australians remain the only Test touring side never to have lost a game in a whole tour. As my father pointed out, the strength of the Australian batting was such that Bill Brown played in only two Tests despite a series of large centuries against the English counties; but he felt that the real difference between the sides was in the bowling. Ray Lindwall was probably the fastest bowler ever seen in England and he had the support of the fiery, penetrative Keith Miller. The stories of Miller's rampant womanising are legion; his talent and athleticism as an all-rounder undisputed. When my father compered a programme on Miller's retirement some years later, Len Hutton called him the most difficult bowler he had ever played against and 'the greatest personality that Australian cricket has ever produced'.

Although Miller was a near-legend in Australia, my father thought his enormous generosity of spirit was not well enough known. Miller was a renowned breaker of stands, seemingly able to pull out something untoward for a batsman totally set. The opposing batsman was public enemy number one. He practically spat at Trevor Bailey in the 1953 series for repeatedly holding up the Australian attack, but off the field he was the first to give Bailey credit for his courage and ability. From that 1948 tour Keith Miller became my father's favourite Australian cricketer, and a friend.

My father's tour of the counties that year also produced

a cherished memory. To most cricket watchers' astonishment, coming to the last game of the season Glamorgan had a chance of winning the County Championship for the first time in their history, but they had to beat Hampshire at Bournemouth and their closest rivals Yorkshire had to fail to beat Somerset at Taunton. Dad was commentating on the Bournemouth match. Wilf Wooller, the Glamorgan captain, was a good friend, as was John Clay, and apart from the obvious fact that Glamorgan were the underdogs my father had a sneaking sentiment for them, perhaps because of the enjoyment of going round Swansea with Dylan Thomas after broadcasting his first matches there. It would mean Hampshire losing; but they had nothing to play for, so he was for Glamorgan.

The course of the game is barely credible by the standards of today and covered wickets. Almost the whole of the first day was lost to rain, and by the start of the final day Hampshire were 50 for 6 in their first innings in reply to Glamorgan's rapidly made 315 all out. Glamorgan needed to take fourteen Hampshire wickets in a short four and three-quarter hour last day.

The Bournemouth wicket is known as a slow turner and Wooller started the last day by bringing on his veteran off-spinner John Clay, who had played in Glamorgan's second-ever match in the Championship twenty-seven years before, and Len Muncer. There was some brief resistance from Leo Harrison and Lofty Herman, but wickets continued to fall to the spinners and Hampshire had to follow on 231 behind when they were all out for 84.

Glamorgan were not the strongest batting or bowling side in the Championship but – ahead of his time in this respect – Wilf Wooller set great store by fielding. At the start of Hampshire's second innings, the opener Arnold hooked and Dyson took a brilliant catch at short leg. Clay and Muncer began to move relentlessly through the Hampshire innings until McCorkell and the Hampshire captain

Desmond Eager came together. Eager began to hit sixes and briefly wrested the initiative until Muncer dispensed with both him and McCorkell to leave Hampshire 101 for 5 at lunch.

The Glamorgan players could barely eat. Victory and the Championship were now a real possibility if Somerset, who were in some trouble themselves, could hold on at Taunton. Forty minutes after lunch Glamorgan had fulfilled their part of the equation, John Clay taking the last wicket as Hampshire were all out for 116. There followed a fraught wait of several hours for the end of the Yorkshire game. When the news came through that Somerset had held out, the large Welsh contingent broke into 'Land of Our Fathers'. The BBC had switched my father's commentary live onto the Welsh service and he could not help but respond to the enormous excitement and pleasure of the Welsh players and supporters at such an unexpected achievement. Years afterwards Welshmen in unlikely climes would come up to him and say they had listened to his commentary that day.

South Africa, Wine and Up the Hill

By the end of the 1948 season my father was established as a commentator. The BBC asked him if he wanted to commentate on his first winter tour – to South Africa for the series of 1948–49. Although he was 34 and had worked for the BBC Overseas Service for several years, apart from a brief services lecture tour of Austria and Italy after the war it was his first trip abroad.

He went out on one of the Castle boats that he had often seen on the beat at night in Southampton. Now he was a passenger travelling first class to be paid to talk about a game he loved. He knew many of the South African players well after their 1947 tour of England, though Alan Melville, the captain of the 1947 side, was to miss most of the series through injury. Despite the stand he would take on the D'Oliveira issue twenty years later, my father was the last to pretend that he did not enjoy the lavish South African hospitality received from many hands. Friends like the South African businessman Wilfred Isaacs were to write accusatory letters over the cancelled 1968 tour. They could not understand that the natural detestation of a liberal for the manifest unfairness of apartheid did not mean that he was trying to deny that he had enjoyed their hospitality.

In 1948 he was not weary enough with travel to fail to enjoy the 'crossing the line' ceremony on the Castle boat or the journey on the Blue train from Cape Town to Johannesburg through the wide-horizoned South African landscape. The cricket was gripping too. The first Test was the closest ever finish at the time. The last eight-ball over provided a grand climax to his first overseas commentary. England's last pair needed one to win off the last ball. In the thickening rain coming in from the Umgeni Hills, Gladwin and Bedser decided to run whatever happened. Gladwin, no batsman, swung and missed. The ball struck his pad and went to short leg where the specks of rain on Tufty Mann's glasses probably decided the affair. By the time he had the ball in his hand the batsmen had scampered home, and moments later Gladwin's strong Derbyshire accent was booming through the English dressing room, 'Coometh the hour, coometh the man.'

Whisky was still a rarity in postwar Britain and the English celebrations were mighty, with no tabloid news reporters on hand to tell tales as the party continued into the night.

If my father had only been interested in cricket he might have become a fan of South Africa, but there was a general election during the tour and he observed the depth of feeling as the Nationalists swept the Smuts government from power and shortly afterwards made apartheid law. When he stopped outside a Nationalist party campaign headquarters on election night with an English-speaking Unionist supporter who made an exclamation of dismay on hearing the latest results, Afrikaaner Nationalist party supporters covered the car windows with spit.

On a rest day from the cricket, he persuaded a bemused coloured taxi driver to take him to one of the townships. It was the first time he had seen Third World poverty in the raw and it made a deep impression. He persuaded one of the England players, S. C. 'Billy' Griffith to go with him on a repeat visit, and although many years later Griffith became Secretary of that generally unthinkingly right-wing body the MCC, he told my father he had never forgotten what they had seen that day.

When Billy Griffith was made wicket-keeper for the fourth Test and Godfrey Evans was dropped, Godfrey – not a man to sit around sulking – insisted that my father, who was his room-mate, accompany him to a highly recommended restaurant well outside Johannesburg. Godfrey borrowed an extremely fast car. It was very late when they finished the meal, which Godfrey used as an excuse to drive even faster on the way back. Dad pointed out that the countryside seemed to be getting less populated and that he thought they were heading even deeper into the Transvaal. Godfrey was of the school who believe 'If we are going to get lost, let's get lost fast', and they covered another five miles before he agreed and they did a U-turn, reaching the hotel as the sun came up.

The trip back to England was to prove as important as anything that happened on the tour. He had booked himself a passage on a flying boat called the 'Speedbird'. It took off from the waters before Cape Town, then turned back over Table Mountain to make its first stop at the Vaal Dam at Johannesburg with dinner and a bed at the Lutjes Langham Hotel.

Such a voyage would have been a luxury any time but in those days not long after the war it was spectacularly so. The flying boat had two floors joined by a deeply carpeted staircase and a comfortable bar on the top floor where they could stand at the counter or sit while enjoying vistas of Africa. Meals and the seating area were downstairs; the night was spent, after dinner, at the landing point.

My father left South Africa for the Zambezi near the Victoria Falls the following morning via a first brush with Afrikaaner officialdom. Afrikaaners were a breed that were progressively gaining lower status on his own list of favoured races. The emigration card even in those pre-apartheid days had an obligatory entry: 'Race – caucasian, native, coloured, mixed, other.' Dad wrote 'Human'.

'Vot's this?' said the Afrikaaner emigration officer.

'It's the race I belong to,' said my father.

'Get on the plane and don't be so bloddy silly.'

The following day it was Lake Victoria and a tribal war dance, then on to the stop he would often recall – the Nile at Luxor; boats with high, graceful sails on the river, many using the same masts as those seen in the paintings on the walls of the catacombs. It was across the river in front of them that the royal dead were taken to the brown and sun-coloured cliffs on their way to the Valley of the Tomb of the Kings. There was a donkey ride from the mooring into Luxor, which it is hard to imagine my father accepting in his later years. There, walking contemplatively along the banks of the Nile in the early evening, he found a small newsstand with a first edition of Cyril Connolly's *The Rock Pool*.

The fifth day was a flight the length of Egypt to tea at Alexandria and then on to Augusta, Sicily. Contemplating his waistline after the scotch, beer and over-indulgence of South Africa, my father asked if it was possible to break his journey. 'Not more than three months or the tickets expire, Sir.'

My father said a week would be more than enough and accepted a recommendation to stay in Taormina, where the flowers would be out. After several days abstinence from alcohol he was losing weight despite the excellent local cuisine when he absent-mindedly poured himself a glass of wine from the jug which stood on every table as a jug of water would in a British guest-house. It tasted good and definitely added to the enjoyment of the food. The seeds of another lifetime enthusiasm had been sown. He took in tow two cheerfully extrovert Americans he found in the bar who were on demobilisation leave, and persuaded them they should find out about wine as well.

The hotelier revealed all he could give under inquisition in English and sent them up the hillside to see his brother, who ran a vineyard. The brother recommended a tour of vineyards round Augusta.

When my mother met my father after the 'Speedbird' had made its final port of call on Southampton Water, there were bottles of wine in his luggage. He announced in his normal moderate way that wine was the only alcoholic drink worth drinking and he would never drink beer or whisky again. He never did.

Sicily and the embryonic love of wine broached other, deeper questions. Maybe the long, conversational Latin family meals were more his style than standing to drink usually with all-male company in British bars. Another new friend via the 'Book of Verse' programme was the novelist Richard Aldington. He had met his wife Netta at a wedding reception – her own wedding reception – and eloped with her only hours later. Aldington had an unusual and powerful personality. He and Netta lived first in Paris and then at Le Lavandou on the Mediterranean coast. Their household was international – often there were Spanish and Italian guests as well as French – and Aldington's influence helped my father question his English small-town attitudes.

His friendship with Richard Aldington was terminated when Netta left him and went to stay first in the Arlott household in London. Perhaps it looked to Richard as though they had taken sides; it was certainly the end of my father's visits to Le Lavandou.

In Dad's youth football had been as much a passion as cricket, so he was pleased when his acceptance as a cricket commentator allowed the chance to commentate on soccer as well. A commentary assignment at Reading was particularly nostalgic, reviving memories of the 35-mile round trip winter evening cycle rides from Basingstoke. Once again his position as commentator allowed access to the dressing room.

Maurice Edelston, the manager's son and a wartime English international, was the attacking star of the postwar Reading side. He had been a schoolmaster and amateur, only turning professional when his father Joe asked him to go to Reading. Maurice was one of the rare breed of thinking footballers. My father found his observations on the game absorbing and hatched the idea of a book called *Wickets, Tries and Goals*. He would write the cricket himself, Maurice the soccer and the Glamorgan captain and ex-Welsh rugby international Wilf Wooller the rugby. It was not a success. He reasoned afterwards that if people want to buy a sports book they want it to be on their favourite sport, and since most people play either rugby or soccer they are not interested in a book examining the finer points of a sport they do not play. However, it was the start of a long friendship with Maurice, whom he was able to steer towards the BBC where Maurice later commentated on football and tennis.

The following summer, 1950, was the year the West Indies came of age as a cricketing nation. My father had enjoyed the way they played cricket since his first sight as a boy of the uniquely elastic Learie Constantine fielding. They had won every series in the Caribbean since England v. West Indies Test matches began, but they had never won a single Test in England. An unlikely pair were to change that and be the talk of the summer – Ramadhin and Valentine. Soon after arriving they unwillingly spent nearly a day on the London underground until they stumbled on an exit by chance – but the English batsmen had the same trouble with their spin as they had had with the map of the underground system.

Both had to be coached in autograph signing on the boat over. Ramadhin was told to include his Christian name.

'What's that?' he asked.

'What did your mother call you?' asked an exasperated senior member of the team.

'Sonny,' he said. 'Sonny' it stayed. He was a tiny Trinidadian Indian with the extraordinary ability of being able to bowl leg-breaks or off-breaks with no discernible change of action. It was not until the following 1957 West Indies tour of England that May and Cowdrey mastered him, when on the advice of the former Yorkshire seam bowler Bill Bowes they played every ball as though it were a leg-break.

Alf Valentine, a Jamaican, was orthodox slow left-arm, but a good one. He took eight wickets on his debut, the first innings of the first Test match. England won, thanks to a record sixth-wicket stand of 161 by Godfrey Evans and Trevor Bailey, but the English cricket authorities were soon to regret their scorn in granting the West Indies only four Tests when they won all the remaining three.

The turning point was the second Test match at Lord's where Ramadhin and Valentine's bowling, helped by centuries from Allan Rae and Clyde Walcott, brought the West Indies' first victory on English soil. The drums and happy, carnival West Indian support were seen on an English cricket ground for the first time and a calypso record was brought out to celebrate the occasion with the refrain, 'With those little pals of mine, Ramadhin and Valentine.' My father bought the record, but it was never mentioned in the family as he would invariably attempt to sing it.

Whenever the 1950 West Indian tour was mentioned, my father would recall an incident that occurred when he was with the West Indians in Derbyshire. He was in the West Indies dressing room when a note was received from someone asking for a brief meeting with the West Indies captain, Clyde Walcott. Ever welcoming, especially in those days when supporters were more respectful, the West Indies invited in the note-writer at the end of play. A tall, pale Derbyshire miner entered the dressing room nervously. He asked if he could meet Clyde Walcott and was directed to him.

'Mr Walcott, my name is also Walcott and I wondered if by any chance we might be re-lay-ted,' he asked in broad Derbyshire.

Clyde Walcott stared friendlily at the man without being able to find the words to broach this interesting prospect when a voice behind him said, 'Don' you stand for that Clyde, man, tell him you's pure African, brother, pure African.'

If the Derbyshire miner was disappointed at having hopes of ancestral links dashed, his nerves and seriousness gradually disappeared as he was given several large rums, departing an hour or so later a West Indies fan.

The additional jobs of cricket and soccer commentating and the books coming off the treadmill were leaving my father little time with the family, but the family finances were becoming increasingly solvent. He had been able to indulge himself a grey AC car to drive back from far-flung cricket grounds, and after the West Indies tour the family moved up the hill from Crouch End to a semi-detached house in the more affluent north London suburb of Highgate. They had just moved in when I was born that winter.

They sold the Barrington Road house to an Irish friend of my mother, Joyce Franks, who had been a nurse with her in Southampton. Joyce was married to a publican and wrote an amusing book about running a pub in Hackney. It was she who coined the nickname for my father of 'The Master'. It was partly affectionate because with the confidence of success behind him he did seem wise and almost all-knowing, and partly mocking because although he achieved his wants politely he was autocratic in the sense that he always knew what he wanted and usually saw to it that he got it. I imagine my father construed it as an affectionate nickname because he used it as the title of a laudatory book he wrote about his favourite cricketer, Jack Hobbs.

As well as the 'Book of Verse' programme, my father enjoyed doing interview programmes during the winter with old cricketers he had found interesting. One he would often quote from was broadcast on Boxing Day that year – an interview with the Surrey and England all-rounder Len Braund. By 1950 Braund had lost both his legs, but he was one of the only two surviving members of the legendary 1902 Manchester Test match against the Australians. He described the agony of the England last man Fred Tate, who had already dropped a crucial catch, shaking like a jelly in the dressing room when the rain came down leaving England with eight to win and one wicket to fall. Tate was partnered by Wilfred Rhodes, but it was Tate to face the bowling when the rain stopped. He snicked a four and was then comprehensively bowled.

Len Braund described the scene in the England dressing room:

> He got into the pavilion with tears in his eyes and he sat down with his head between his hands.
>
> 'Well, Fred, old boy,' I said, 'you mustn't be down-hearted about that. You'll drop some more before you're finished.'
>
> He said, 'Oh no, Len, it will never be forgotten, never be forgotten. He said, 'I didn't get anything of the runs I should have got and I've been and dropped the catch.'
>
> He said to me, 'What am I to do? What are they going to think of me when I get home?'
>
> I said, 'They'll think nothing about you, it's only a memory of a few days; in two or three weeks they'll forget all about it.'
>
> 'No they won't,' said Fred, 'they'll always remember me for it.' And of course they have.
>
> 'Don't worry,' I said, 'go and get your money. It's only a game.'

Then we start off at the end of the game, we went to the station and I think we just went in and had a glass of beer. Tried to cheer him up but there was no cheering him up. And we get into the train and he looked very mournful.

'I've let England down but I've got someone at home, a little boy, who will come along and make good all my failures in this match.'

Well, the great Maurice [Tate] come along into the English side, and I don't suppose I've ever seen a greater bowler in the history of cricket. Poor old Fred has had his wish as far as Maurice is concerned.

That was it, what a game it was, what a wicket and what players. More than twenty years afterwards Maurice was making up for what his father had done when he dropped that catch and didn't get those runs. So you see in a way that Test match lasted more than twenty years. But now there's only two of us left, only me and Wilfred. But I don't think anybody will ever forget that Test match.

The sentiment my father would often quote from that monologue of Len Braund's was not the happy ending with Maurice Tate, although he was a big fan of Maurice's, but Len Braund's 'Go and get your money. It's only a game.'

It would occur to him in his annual tour around the counties. Over the years he saw too many men he liked agonising about whether they could keep their place, or put an end to a bad run. While he fully appreciated that they were professionals and it was a matter of livelihood, he increasingly felt there was not enough 'Go and get your money. It's only a game.'

After his first tentative contacts while a policeman, the BBC literature producer's job also enabled my father to get to know John Betjeman. He admired Betjeman's poems –

his own poetry was somewhat in the Betjeman style, though not as talented or amusing, as he knew. They also shared a love of architecture and country churches.

As is well known from his television performances as well as his poetry, Betjeman had a fine sense of humour and an original mind. When he invited my parents down to Berkshire, he would laugh with my mother at my father's inability to handle his wife, Lady Penelope. The daughter of the Commander-in-Chief in India, Field Marshal Lord Chetwode, Lady Penelope loved riding and with her no-nonsense upper-class manner would insist on my father helping to 'muck out' the horses or feed her pet goat. My father had no knowledge of or interest in this side of country life. He was also quite a natty dresser at the time and he would sadly run a finger down the well-pressed creases of his light beige corduroys before departing with Lady Penelope. His joy would not be increased by seeing John and my mother, scotch-in-hand, doubled up with mirth watching his activity in the stables from the safety of the sitting room.

In 1950 there was another major change. Jim Penne-thorne-Hughes was made Head of the BBC Staff Training School and he offered a job as instructor to my father. It would mean the end of the 'Book of Verse' and the other literary programmes, but it ensured the relaxation and freedom of working for someone who was a personal friend. It meant moving office, and the Corporation provided him with a new secretary, Valerie France, the daughter of a Bromley doctor.

The new job entailed my father having to take the chair at expert lectures. A lot of the talk involved broadcasting techniques that he had used naturally. It was like a musician who had learnt 'by ear' being taught to read music, but he discovered a lot about the techniques of broadcasting while trying to impart it to others.

More importantly, working for Jim Pennethorne-Hughes allowed him to accept any other offers that came his way. The editor of the London *Evening News*, John Marshall, asked my father if he would write a weekly column. They got to like each other and, knowing my father liked wine, John Marshall asked him if he could recommend a good imitation champagne for his son's christening party. Just the week before, a wine merchant had told my father he was about to import a new sparkling Languedoc which was one of the first champagne imitations to go on sale in Britain.

When one of the *Evening News* directors asked John Marshall at the end of the party the name of the excellent champagne they had been drinking, John told him he would send him the details and asked my father if he would like to write a food and drink column. This might have seemed a daunting project for someone who could not cook and had only tasted his first glass of wine in Sicily a few years before, but help was at hand.

My father's name was added to the list of Fleet Street wine columnists, and he was immediately invited on a press tour of the Saint-Emilion region. My father booked a holiday at the same time when my mother, who also liked wine, agreed to go. He was boasting about his forthcoming holiday in front of Laurence Gilliam, Head of BBC Features. Gilliam said he was going to Saint-Emilion after the written press tour to do a BBC Features programme with André Simon as expert and Wynford Vaughan-Thomas as broadcaster, and he suggested my father could do some colour pieces.

The most hospitable and knowledgeable chatelain on the press tour was Daniel Querre of Château Monbousquet. My father was seduced by the leisurely pace of life in inland Gironde, where every waking heartbeat of practically every inhabitant is dominated by growing, bottling, selling and drinking wine.

This is my father's account of his first meeting with
Daniel Querre, which was printed in the *Adelphi* magazine:

We waited for Daniel Querre in the courtyard of the
Hôtel de Plaisance in the Gironde wine town of Saint-
Emilion. The usual visitors to Saint-Emilion are vint-
ners, concerned with the surrounding wine-growing châteaux rather than with the town itself: but there are
others, outriders from the main touring army – the
church fancier, the rubber of brasses, the connoisseur of
rood screens or the student of ecclesiastical history.
These, since they belong by nature to the fabric of such
a place, leave it uninvaded and the full caravan of
tourism does not enter Saint-Emilion. The town could
not contain it. At such threat of commerce, there would
be panic in the little house-shops which religiously
display the original macarons, yet do so, it seems, more
out of respect for tradition than from hope of real profit.
The tread of so many strange feet would choke the
thousand-year monastery town with the dust of its dead
prelates, and the pulse of the impatient touring motorcar
stream through the narrow streets and tiny squares
would burst those age-hardened arteries. Thus, there is
in Saint-Emilion no alien noise – which is the only really
disturbing form of noise. Its sounds are the native
sounds, which are part of the pattern of quietness.

We waited for Daniel Querre when even the usual
church-front loungers were away at the grape harvest,
leaving the Place to a stillness in which waiting became
intransitive, a state of grace. Above us the bell of Saint-
Emilion simultaneously marked and mocked the passage
of time. Out of compassion for centuries of those who
sleep late for mass, it strikes the hour a full two minutes
ahead of the hands of the clock: but, with equal compassion for clockmakers, strikes it again, punctually upon
the hour.

At a table there the contents of a glass are as enjoyable
contemplated as drunk. Behind, the firm, grey ecclesiast-

ical walls promise eternal rest. The bell tower climbs from our side eighty feet into the air, and its far more ancient monolithic chapel is directly beneath your feet. So the floor is a roof, this green wooden café table a look-out tower. Beyond the low courtyard wall, the V of the immediate houses carves a sharp gulf, and the vineyards which run as far as the horizon are, even at their nearest, more dimly distant than their distance. The light is solicitous to protect the eye from the search for detail: even at full sunshine the lines of the houses are smudged to a crayon softness. Though it is early afternoon and no mist rises, there is an impression of haze over this stretch of the Gironde, where every mile has named a bottle.

I believe that Daniel Querre's sense of the contemplation induced by the Plaisance courtyard prompts him to appoint his meetings there. A man who is always late for appointments must be either shameless, or thus imaginative in his choice of such a meeting place. It has one further advantage as a rendezvous for the latecomer; those waiting for him are conscious of his approach – and so cease to account him late – a full ten minutes before his arrival. The imperious horn of Daniel Querre's long, French car is to be heard several kilometres away. He refuses to recognise travelling time between one activity and the next, but he is indignantly intolerant of any check. He drives with a characteristically French estimate of safe speed and margins of clearance, but with due consideration for children, women, animals and men in that order. Level-crossings, on the other hand, rouse him to an ecstasy of anger. Let him find the gates closed against him and he begins his address to the crossing keeper as he applies the brake and continues it, from the middle of the road with the contemptuous gestures at the passing train, until the gates open again – when he immediately gives precedence to a hobbling farm-cart.

His car cries in top gear up the one-cart-width hill of St Emilion and swings into the Place with a glorious disregard for centrifugal force. Then he is with you – even as he leaves his car, twenty yards away, to walk to your table. Although one leg drags a little from some old foot injury, he seems to swallow walking distances in a movement. He is heavily square in build but, in the flick of the small dark eyes in his wine-and-weather red face and the uprush of his short black hair, there is a quick, eager note. A spread of his hands conveys an embrace to everyone. A look, a containing sweep of the arms, admits an entire concourse to his affection. No need to call for the waitress; she, hitherto elusive, is at his side waiting for his order. Now an apéritif. Next, lunch: the meal ordered for an hour ago has, at this moment, been completed. The rich, dark dish of lampreys is smoking on the table. The wine is from our host's own cellar, for this is an occasion. To Daniel Querre every meal is an occasion, bringing food and wine and people and conversation; lacking one of these ingredients, it would not be a meal – not an occasion. Above all the occasion of his finest setting is dinner at his own château: he will take lunch anywhere within a hundred miles, but his dinner is only properly to be taken at home.

At the strong square table of his own château, Daniel Querre is, unmistakably, a great lord, the grower, maker and giver of wine. When he bought Château Monbousquet with almost all his money, he dedicated the latter half of his life to raising its wine again to the high peak which is eminence among the great clarets. It is a long, slow process, this digging up of meagre vines, the ten fallow years of long planted ground, the slow, fifteen-year coming of new vines to maturity. There are summers – all too frequent – when a single ill-timed frost, a single week of rain, will reduce a great vintage – for all that any man may do – to a mediocre one. After the pressing of the wine and the maturing years in barrel before bottling, there are years – no one can foretell how many – before it comes to its greatest in bottle. These anxieties Daniel Querre embraced with the zeal of one entering a life of devotion.

Shall we return for dinner? But yes – there will be two guests-four guests-six guests-eight guests. There is no telephone at Monbousquet. As we drive along the gravel road and under the arch, the car is not going anywhere, it is coming home quietly. The Jersey cream wall of the château runs its shutter-windowed length beside the drive, looking down on the lake where the bullfrogs grunt. Madame Querre is at the door: there is accustomed and easy affection between husband and wife at seeing one another. 'How many guests?' 'Dinner will not be long.' Room gives on room: there are apéritifs, armchairs: a friend painted those pictures which capture the attention. There is a family to meet, a family interested in itself and in its guests. The château ceases to be merely an architectural delight: it is a family. The head of the family sits down to the dinner table with his wife, his two sons – both bright, dark-eyed and quick in response as their father – with the daughter of the brother whom the Gestapo treated characteristically and tragically, the son of a distant cousin studying the vine as an agriculturist, and with his friends. He eats with a catholic and critical enjoyment and drinks with a round, uncomplicated delight founded on knowledge and a palate which he does not allow tobacco to dull. The wines of the other châteaux of Bordeaux come to him with the automatic courtesy of one wine-grower to another, and he tastes them with critical gratitude. He takes his holidays and other periodical visits in Burgundy so that, on those two – the greatest – wine districts, he is an authority.

Always the formula with a glass of wine is the same; in an Englishman it can hardly but appear affected, but with the Frenchman of wine it is a reflex. Holding the wine glass by the foot, he surveys the wine reflectively against the light. Then, quietly, he brings the glass towards his nose, rotating it by the foot until the wine rises in a racing wave to precisely the height of rim. Then, having thus washed the air in wine, he savours the bouquet. The drinking becomes the third, and the greatest, of the taster's pleasures. Asked his opinion of the wine, such a man rarely uses terms of 'good' or 'bad'.

For him it is sufficient to agree with the label – say a Château Latour 1939. That is sufficient. It means that the wine has all the normal attributes of a Château Latour wine – and they are practically invariable – blended with the characteristic of the year – 1939 – whose weather, with that of every other year, every French wine expert knows automatically.

Daniel Querre reaches under his chair. The wine bottles are there. This bottle bears his own label – Château Monbousquet. The picture on the label is of the house in which we sit: in the centre of the picture is the window of the room where we are dining. Of courtesy the châtelain takes the first taste, a little in his wine glass to ascertain and to demonstrate that it is fit hospitality for his guests. If it were not for business, he says, he would never leave this château, never drink any wine but his own Monbousquet. The enthusiast looks at his enthusiasm against the light. Gravely, almost sternly, he ascertains that the scent is as he would have it. He tastes it and his pride is confirmed. Across his own table, he pours his own wine for his guests.

When my father told Daniel Querre cheerfully that after his tour as *Evening News* wine correspondent he would be back in a month with the BBC, Daniel said, 'Why go back?' and suggested my father spend the intervening month at Château Monbousquet as his guest.

Daniel was responsible for public relations of Saint-Emilion wines and one of the Fleet Street wine correspondents on the tour told a story about him. Soon after the war Daniel was hosting a group of American wine buyers in Paris and for entertainment one evening they asked him if he could identify three wines they had chosen. The first magnum – they chose magnums so that all the buyers could taste a glass of the same wine – was poured for Daniel by the head waiter of the hotel with the napkin over the label. Daniel held the glass up to the light, swirled it round, sniffed it and slowly swilled it round his mouth. Leisurely he announced it was a great Bordeaux, a Château Latour, a Château Latour 1926. The label was revealed and the American buyers were impressed.

The second magnum was brought. He took longer over this one. He held it to the light, sniffed it and pronounced it 'not of his region', a Burgundy and a famous Burgundy; he was not so good on Burgundy but he would think it was a Chambertin, he would guess a Clos de Bèze, old – but not quite so old as the first, perhaps 1929. It was a Clos de Bèze 1929.

The waiter brought the third magnum in a rapt silence. Daniel went through the usual tasting routine and said he was certain of this one. It was of his region and he had had the good fortune to taste it many times. It was a Cheval Blanc 1924. The American buyers applauded generously and Daniel Querre sold many cases of Saint-Emilion wines.

On the second week of his stay when they were alone at the end of the meal, my father plucked up the courage to ask if the story were true. Daniel's eyes twinkled.

'It is a true story but it is not so clever as it sounds. Of course I do not know all red wines and getting the year correct is a very chancy matter even for an expert, but it was not so difficult in this case because I chose the hotel and they only have three wines in magnums.'

My father had the luck to be at Château Monbousquet during the *vendange*. He loved the way each château took pride in the way they fed the harvesters and the smoothly efficient way Madame Querre ran the château with no telephone yet never turning a hair at any number of last-minute guests. My father was convinced that this was the ideal way to live and he became fond of doing the same thing, but Madame Querre had an advantage over my mother and later my stepmothers – she had a team of local helpers as well as an unlimited supply of wine in the cellar.

By the time the month's stay at Château Monbousquet

was over my father had observed and questioned enough, with the help of practically every English-language wine book in his bedroom, to understand most of what André Simon was talking about when he arrived.

Wine, however, had yet to take off in Britain. Package trips to Spain when more English people began to taste wine had not begun. It remained primarily an indulgence of the rich, so after a year or so of his 'Table Talk' column John Marshall changed my father's brief to writing a column about whatever took his fancy, entitled 'It occurs to me'. Whatever it was that was to occur to Dad usually occurred only in the last possible hour before the piece was to go to print. The columns are a mishmash – from memories of a pork butcher in Basingstoke to Dad's system of doing the pools – but one piece stands out: his obituary to the *Evening News* columnist Ian Mackay.

> Tonight I looked in his usual corner for Ian Mackay. He was not there. Often in the past I have looked and if I did not see or hear him I would wonder casually where he was this particular evening – in what town, county, country or continent.
>
> Tonight it was different because this time he will not be back. That evening eleven days ago he was Ian Mackay as we all knew him. Then in a few minutes he was gone. That perhaps is how he would wish it for he could never bear to live his life anything but fully and widely.
>
> He was, you will know – and may prove merely by reading his essays – a very fine writer. As a talker he was every bit as good. There are men labelled as good talkers who run on and on spilling occasional brilliance into a canal of monologue. Ian Mackay was a good talker all the time because he was a good listener. He was a Scot from Wick and one of the few things with which he was

careful was speech: he valued it too much to allow it to become dross.

Memory of some people recalls their face and little more. Of Ian Mackay it recalls greying hair which could never be barbered out of a suggestion of shagginess: he obviously never wasted good living time on the nicer points of knotting a tie, nor did he mind if the points of his collar stuck out on different planes.

He had a jaw which was strong: it could be more than that, because on certain humane arguments he admitted of no argument: yet his mouth – almost always – and his eyes – always – held humour. Sometimes he wore his false teeth, sometimes not: it did not matter: he was bigger than appearances. He had a steady regard.

Yet we shall remember the look of him less than we shall recall the pitch of his voice and its eager inflection. We shall remember at odd moments a hundred facets of his talk – Ranji's glass eye, an Alsatian wine, a suggested gloss of Shakespeare, a deliberate and masterly misquotation, a single sentence which punctured a pretentious contemporary.

Everything was grist to the mill of his mind, but catholic as he was in his interests, he was never gullible. He had a wide and easy tolerance and strict standards: his sense of humour and his sense of justice were interwoven: there were few moments of his fifty-three years that he would count as wasted. Ian Mackay was a man who lived in three dimensions.

Like most of his best writing and broadcasting about other people, this piece includes phrases which unconsciously applied as much to my father as to the person he was writing about. 'He was careful with speech: he valued it too much to allow it to become dross.' My father not only tried not to use clichés in his own writing and broadcasts, he was actually pained if someone suggested a cliché or used one. His mind endlessly searched for a

The old cemetery lodge, Basingstoke,
where John Arlott was born in 1914

Jack Arlott

John Arlott with his mother Nellie

Aged 17

Policeman, Southampton

Dawn, Jim, John and Tim Arlott
at home in Highgate Avenue, London

Radio producer

The young poet

In the studio. *Left to right:* Hugh Metcalfe, John Arlott, Preston Lockwood, George Robey, James McKechnie, Dylan Thomas, Robin Holmes

Cricket commentary at Scarborough, 1946

With Denis Compton on England's 1948–49 tour of South Africa

Dawn Arlott, with Jim and Tim

Jim Arlott, at 19

With Valerie and Robert at
The Old Sun, Alresford, 1966

correct and exact description of what he was seeing or wanted to say.

As far as commentary technique went, my father always imagined he was not speaking to millions of listeners but to someone on their own sitting at home – perhaps his mother or someone who did not know about cricket, who needed to have it carefully and enthusiastically explained. That person would be as interested to know not just about the play but about what it was like to be watching the cricket at Hove that particular morning – 'the blue seaside sky, the white wedding-cake grandstand and the sea mist nine-tenths gone from the ground like Tenniel's Cheshire cat.'

Sports columnist Bill McGowran shared Dad's room at the *Evening News*. Bill was a Sherlock Holmes enthusiast and a member of the Sherlock Holmes Society. To his nervous excitement he once succeeded in getting a titled and renowned Sherlock Holmes expert, who had avoided joining the society, to address one of its regular dinners. Bill was nervous because he would have to make the introductory speech and he did not like public speaking. The dinner was to be in the 'Wig and Pen' club in Fleet Street and Bill was to collect his guest. He had neatly typed out his speech days before and had left a piece he had had stockpiled a long while for that day's column. Foolishly, as it transpired, he decided to take the rest of the day off.

My father in his wine enthusiasm had been working on weening Bill away from bitter and Bill had recently decided that he quite liked a schooner or two of medium sherry. He went to check that all the arrangements were in place at the 'Wig and Pen'. Being away from his usual drinking partners and feeling in animated holiday spirits with the afternoon off, he also decided to try a shot from the interesting-looking green bottle on the top shelf called Crème de Menthe. To his sweet palate it tasted good. Indeed, he made a determined effort to make Dad try one as he passed by with some dinner guests on his way back to the *Evening News*, but my father had not yet started on an overdue piece – too bad. Bill sank back into the comfortable armchair, taking another couple of glasses of Crème de Menthe as he leisurely read the afternoon's paper. There were two more hours to kill before he fetched his guest from Euston station. He felt a little muzzy as he stood up to leave, but some cold water in the face and a glass of lemonade and he would be all right. Anyway there would be an enforced gap of an hour while he fetched the guest and he would stick to just half of a pint of his usual tipple in the pre-dinner drinks.

There were late-comers and the pre-dinner drinks went on longer than expected, but finally everyone was seated. They were halfway through the first course when Bill was suddenly and violently sick, so sick that friends had to take him away from the dinner and home in a taxi. Bill never heard his celebrated guest's speech. It was the Sherlock Holmes Society not the Hellfire Club, and word of Bill's unsuccessful evening had spread far by the time he turned up for work the following day looking greyer than usual.

Heads were down low over typewriters with less of the usual idle chat until my father asked Bill if he thought Portsmouth had a chance in that night's midweek game against Arsenal.

Bill paused before reflecting, 'There was something wrong with that bloody fish soup, you know.'

My father's position as General Instructor of the BBC Staff Training School helped bring offers his way – one was to join the commentary team for the Coronation. He was not much of a royalist. When I was 12, I asked him, 'What do you think about the royal family, Dad?'

'I don't think about them,' he replied. But in 1953 he was happy enough to be on the commentary team for such an event and his native cunning for having the most comfortable commentary position was becoming evident.

As the reporters stood in the rain taking the opinion of the crowd, Dad had had his commentary position set up in the restaurant of the Criterion Hotel overlooking Piccadilly Circus. The menu was always available. As the Coronation procession wound slowly past, the Duke of Beaufort, who had met my father at the rehearsal, looked up at the restaurant where my father was topping up a glass of claret and remarked to Viscount Alanbrooke next to him, 'That lucky young devil Arlott is sitting up there with a bottle of wine while we're doing this.'

The Coronation was in the middle of the remarkable cricket season when England won back the Ashes from the Australians. The 1–0 series result sounds unexciting, but my father had had the superb second Test at Lord's to commentate on when Trevor Bailey, with 71 in four and three-quarter hours, and Willie Watson resisted Lindwall and Miller at their most furious, epitomising the bulldog spirit for a generation of English supporters. They held out for a draw when defeat had seemed certain; and, courtesy of Laker and Lock, England won the final Test which was extended to six days for a result. It was a victory greeted by much emotion, the first time England had won the Ashes at home since 1926.

That winter my father organised the first of three annual lunches he launched in his lifetime. In the way that boyhood heroes can never be bettered in the memory of any man, Jack Hobbs of Surrey and England was his favourite cricketer. It was not his amazing record or even the faultless technique which so stirred my father's admiration as Jack Hobbs's attitude. From the first Test match he had watched at the Oval when he was 12, my father had carried a picture in his mind of Hobbs laughing with genuine good heart at the Australian spin bowler Arthur Mailey when – rarest of occurrences – he bowled Hobbs with a slow full toss. He was the consummate professional, and yet at the same time Len Braund never had to tell Jack Hobbs, 'It's only a game.'

The friendship with Jack Hobbs which BBC commentary had afforded my father was the most cherished. For several years he had had lunch with him next to Hobbs's sports shop in Fleet Street at the Wellington Restaurant, kept by a Belgian called Emil Haon. My father admired Hobbs's gentle modesty and shyness and in 1953 on the spur of the moment with John Marshall, Kenneth Adam and Alf Gover it was decided to hold an annual lunch called the Master's lunch on Jack Hobbs's birthday, 16 December. 1953 was also Hobbs's 70th birthday, and my father arrived for the lunch with a poem written in tribute to him.

> There falls across this one December day
> The light remembered from those suns of June
> That you reflected, in the summer play
> Of perfect strokes across the afternoon.
>
> No yeoman ever walked his household land
> More sure of step or more secure of lease
> Than you, accustomed and unhurried, trod
> Your small, yet mighty, manor of the crease.
>
> The game the Wealden rustics handed down
> Through growing skill became, in you, a part
> Of sense; and ripened to a style that showed
> Their country sport matured to balanced art.
>
> There was a wisdom so informed your bat
> To understanding of the bowler's trade,
> That each resource of strength or skill he used
> Seemed but the context of the stroke you played.
>
> The Master: records prove the title good;
> Yet figures fail you, for they cannot say
> How many men whose names you never knew
> Are proud to tell their sons they saw you play.

They share the sunlight of your summer day
Of thirty years; and they, with you, recall
How, through those well wrought centuries,
Your hand reshaped the history of bat and ball.

The club grew in numbers, mostly those who had known Hobbs or played with him. After Emil died and the Wellington Restaurant closed, the annual lunch eventually moved to the Oval on the suggestion of Raman Subba Row.

Long after Jack himself had died and my father was too tired and feeble for public engagements or annual events, he would still make the journey to London for the Master's lunch, which is still held. My father was keen for it to continue. Whether it can or should make the transition from a meal with those who played with Jack Hobbs or knew him to those for whom he can only stand as a grand figure of cricket, however hard they try to conjure up his spirit, remains to be seen.

By 1954 my father was a regular member of the panel of the radio programme 'Any Questions'. His views on South Africa were already getting him into deep waters. He spoke his mind forcefully as ever when there was a question on apartheid, and the matter was raised at the BBC Monday morning conference with the Director-General. A defender volunteered that my father had said nothing stronger than the Liberal peer Lady Violet Bonham-Carter had already done on another programme. Unaware of the total freedom of my father's working arrangements with Jim Penne-thorne-Hughes at the BBC Staff Training School, and thinking of his weekly column in the *Evening News*, the Director-General said, 'It's not as if he were still on the staff, is it?'

His detractors pointed out that he was indeed still on the staff. The Director-General ruled that since a member of BBC staff should not be allowed on any programme where he could express editorial opinion, my father should be taken off the staff but allowed to continue on any programme on which he was wanted on a total annual income not less than he had earned as a member of staff. Dad lamented the loss of his safe BBC pension but retained a soft spot for the organisation ever after because of their reasonable treatment of him – and many freelance opportunities were beckoning. It meant renting a room in his accountant's offices off Charing Cross Road. He asked his efficient secretary, Valerie France, if she wanted to come with him and she accepted.

Fuelled by feedback from his political utterances on 'Any Questions' and encouraged by his mother, my father then became involved in politics. When the Epping Liberal Association on the north-east corner of the London suburbs and their agent Norman Hoddell asked him if he would stand as Liberal candidate for them at the next elections, he agreed. The Conservatives were in power. Squeezed by the Labour vote, and with no dramatic by-election victories to bolster support, the Liberals were at the nadir of their power. Outside a few strongholds the pinnacle of their ambitions was to save their deposit, so my father did not contemplate the possibility of having to turn in his blooming freelance living for the unbolstered pay of a Liberal MP. Anyway, before any election prospect lay the offer of commentating for the BBC on the English cricket side's tour of Australia.

The main talking point of the preceding English cricket season was the arrival of the first genuinely fast bowler England had had since before the war – Frank Tyson.

Dad's friend the Hampshire wicket-keeper Leo Harrison told him the favourite story in the county dressing-rooms. Word spreads fast among professional cricketers when someone new and genuinely fast arrives. The sides who had played Northamptonshire spoke of this balding fellow who bowled off a short run but could be terrifyingly quick.

Jim Sims, the Middlesex leg-spin bowler, was getting bored of hearing such tales. One evening in the Lord's bar, as one of the opposing side was telling the listening circle that the Warwickshire boys had said that Tyson was even quicker than they thought he would be, he could bear it no longer. 'Tyson,' he said, 'I could play him with my cock.'

The company pondered the prospect in silence. Middlesex were not due to play Northants until early September. When they did, Northants went in first and made about 300, leaving themselves with an hour to bowl at Middlesex in fading light at the end of the day – a time for maximum effort from Tyson, especially on a ground where Test selectors were likely to be watching.

After forty minutes Middlesex were 18 for 3. Walter Robins, the captain, who had been bowled by Tyson for one, returned aggressively to the dressing room, threw his bat on the floor and said, 'Get your dick out, Jim, you're in next.'

My father and Frank Tyson became close pals. He once talked Frank through 'a bad patch' on Burgundy at Highgate Avenue until the small hours of the morning, packing him into his car at dawn to drive back to Northampton for the following morning's game. Before the lunch break at the game my father was covering he received a telegram: 'Burgundy works – 4 for 1, Frank.'

My father adored cheese, and he had another job before the Australian tour – a commissioned book about cheeses for the English Country Cheese Council. He naturally chose his favourite regions – the south, the south-west and Wales – to write about Cheddar, Double Gloucester, Caerphilly and Blue Vinny, a little-known Dorset cheese that was the find of the tour as far as Dad was concerned. He had this to say about it for the Cheese Council:

> The miracle is the 'blue'. Dorset is full of stories, some
> by no means appetising, of the means employed of old to

set up the veining. Without it, Dorset is an unpleasant cheese with a dirty, earthy taste. It was said that the blue ate up that bad flavour and replaced it with its own, completely different taste. Men will tell you, around Sherborne, that on the farms which produced the finest Dorset Blue, the carters used to dip the harness leathers in the milk churn when they came in at night; and how old harnesses, and even old boots, were left in the dairy. In fact this has a good scientific basis, for the blue mould grows rapidly on damp leather.

Modern creameries have inoculated cheeses with the mould spores of penicillium roqueforti – which is the blueing agent; but the result is not the same, and no scientist claims that it is. Natural blue takes anything up to nine months to grow inside the cheese; no laboratory can match that slow harmonious growth in time with the full ripening process.

Dorset folk will tell you that the best Blue Vinny was matured for eighteen months, often, for a third of that time at the bottom of a vat of cider – which cleared the cider and ripened the cheese. Spoilt Blue Vinny is as hard as a cartwheel and more than once has been used as a cheese in a skittle alley. Eaten, it will induce a thirst not to be quenched by any normal quantity of drink.

Of all the cheeses still made it is the hardest to find, but it is worth the search. It is amazing that a skimmed milk cheese should be so noble and round and rich, without a trace of the pungency we find in so much of the Continental blues.

No man – Dorset Blue Vinny is essentially a male taste – with a relishing palate should die without having tasted the Vinny. Take a piece of dry bread, crisp dry, even hard dry like a Dorset Knob. Spread Blue Vinny carefully, and certainly not very thickly over it. You need nothing with it; chew it slowly. The bouquet will remain with you – subtle yet round – long after you have swallowed it, and you will remember for much longer than that.

My father believed his own advertising copy. For twenty years afterwards he would make detours on drives back from cricket matches to get a whole Dorset Blue and the hard Dorset Knob rolls, except that he never had it with 'nothing', always a glass or two of red wine.

Australia

My father did not like Australia. In 1954–55 the sophisticating wave of Italian, Yugoslav and other European and Asian immigrants was yet to arrive and there was nothing to divert the national psyche from the obsession of beating 'the Poms'. My father was also in the artificial position of travelling with an English cricket side who were expected to lose but had forgotten the script. The depth of feeling aroused by a cricket tour of Australia by 'the Poms' can only be appreciated by those who have experienced it. An England soccer side playing at Hampden have an idea, but that experience lasts only a few hours whereas a cricket tour of Australia goes on for months of either preening Australian victory or what is seen as national humiliation.

More particularly to the outrage of Australian virility in 1954–55 the spectacular fast bowlers were no longer Lindwall and Miller, who had butchered the Poms in 1948 and threatened them in 1953, but England's Tyson and Statham. Winning or losing, there is a siege mentality in a touring team abroad – a feeling that the whole country from chambermaid to Prime Minister is against you. In Australia they are.

Then, for my father, there was the weather. The air shimmering off Brisbane's Gabba pitch as the temperature broke into the 100s provoked dreams of a cool Atlantic westerly coming off the Bristol Channel at Mumbles in September. The suggestion of spending a day in the superb Pacific rollers or, worse, 'sun-baking' would have brought a deep frown of distaste. Worse still, the Australian wine industry, which has since developed into a force to be reckoned with, was still flexing its muscles in 1954 when like his British counterpart the average Australian thought only of beer.

My father took a flat with the former Yorkshire seam bowler and cricket journalist Bill Bowes in Sydney's King's Cross, then a rakish area which he quite enjoyed. Unfortunately he recommended it to me twenty years later when it had become a haunt of transvestites, pimps and prostitutes.

Nor were the fiercely egalitarian Sydney taxi drivers my father's cup of tea. If you were travelling with a friend and both sat in the back instead of one in front next to the driver he would greet you with, 'What's a matter, mite, do I smell or something?'

My father found Sydney attractive. No one could fail to be impressed by the open airiness of the wide harbour and bridge, but he greatly enjoyed Fred Trueman's remark to a Sydney cabbie on a later tour. When the cabbie asked Fred, 'What do you think of our bridge, Mr Trueman?' Fred replied, 'Your bridge, your bridge, what do you mean your bridge? It was built by a Yorkshire firm, Dorman and Long, and you buggers haven't finished paying for it yet.'

From the first Test match, which was disastrous from the English point of view, no one could have guessed what would happen during the rest of my father's only Australian tour. Len Hutton, who had already been the target of much criticism after being appointed England's first professional captain, won the toss and put Australia in to bat – something which no English captain in Australia had ever done before. It would be a long time before one did it again. Australia made 601 for 8 declared and reduced England to 21 for 4. To make matters worse, England's star batsman Denis Compton broke his hand on a post behind the boundary while fielding. Cowdrey and Bailey in the first innings and Edrich and May in the second made token gestures, but Australia won by an innings.

The Australian captain, Ian Johnson, was injured before the second Test. Arthur Morris was made captain, and in a push for psychological supremacy he put England in. The gamble looked to have paid off when England were out for 154. Australia were 88 for 2 at lunch on the second day before Tyson started to show his venom. He and Trevor Bailey took four wickets each and, although the match continued close, England eventually won by 38 runs.

The third Test was also close until the fourth innings. Needing 240 to win, the Australians were 75 for 2 when the final day began. In the book he wrote at the time, *Australian Test Journal*, my father called it 'as exciting and moving a day's play' as he had ever seen.

There was scandal in the air, and in the English and Australian press, because of English accusations that someone had watered the Melbourne wicket during the weekend. The wide cracks visible on the pitch on the Saturday evening had mysteriously closed up by the Monday morning, although there had been no rain. An official denial did not kill the story.

As play began, my father was talking to several members of the 1926 Australian side that toured England. In this Test, England had got the wickets they had taken mainly through spin and there was a consensus among the old Australian players that the Melbourne pitch would not help faster bowlers. My father turned from the conversation just in time to see Harvey attempt to glance Tyson down the leg side, get a faint touch and be caught by Godfrey Evans. Tyson then bowled Benaud and had Miller caught to have figures of 3 for 4, accounting for the heart of the Australian batting. He proceeded to turn his figures into 6 for 16. Statham was fast and accurate at the other end and the Australians faded to 111 all out to give England the Ashes and the tour party a mighty celebration.

The fourth Test in Adelaide in 100 degree heat brought another victory for England – and a brush with a waiter in the pavilion restaurant. My father had been trying to taste a recommended South Australian red wine. The waiter had scowled when my father asked for it during the earlier South Australian state game. When my father had persisted, saying it was a local wine and that he would be back for the Test match, the waiter had finally agreed to write the name down and said he would have it for the Test match. Seating my father at the table during the first lunch break of the Test match, he said, 'I've got yer wine, mite', leant forward conspiratorially and hissed, 'And it's well iced.'

Another reason my father had an unpleasant overall memory of Australia was simply that he was homesick. For the first time in his new life the excitement of work and seeing new countries was beginning to pall. He was not just away for the cricket tour. He had arranged with the *Evening News* that he would write articles about Pakistan, Hong Kong, Japan and Korea on the journey out and Fiji, Hawaii, San Francisco, Chicago and New York on the way back, so he was away for more than six months in all.

In a note to Valerie, his secretary, he wrote: 'It is Christmas Eve – about midnight and I am at John Wilkes' house feeling a little maudlin. I have talked to them at home tonight and Timothy cried and that so shook me that I am foolishly homesick. I suppose I am too old to leave home and come across the world.'

He gave his brief views on Australia in the same letter to Valerie.

Australia is bright, brash, noisy but friendly but the country is all the same. They are nice people but there is no variety. I have a fancy to write a book about Australia. The Australians would hate it but I would be out of the country by then.

I have been having a wonderful time on 'Any Questions' out here: they think I am dynamite – me! – a sort of antipodean visiting Gilbert Harding. I get very high before the programme and talk about sex: it seems to work. They have asked me to be on the programme every week until I leave, then America and then home; and that cannot be too soon.

His book on the series, written in the Sydney flat he had rented, is dedicated 'To Jimmy and Timothy, wishing they were here to interrupt my writing with their mischief' – and I think he meant it.

However, I know it was not all sackcloth and ashes. Enjoying a party with Dad's friends John and Betty Wilkes in the opulent north Sydney suburb of Chinaman's Bay twenty years later, I left the swimming pool with a young lady and disappeared deep into their large back garden. I was disturbed when a loud voice through a megaphone interrupted proceedings: 'Timothy Arlott, there are funnel-web spiders in that garden.' John tittered about this after I had returned sheepishly to the house with the young lady, and when I asked him why he found it so funny, he replied, 'I used this megaphone to shout the same words at your father in the same circumstances twenty years ago.'

Of course, the cricket tours of South Africa and Australia were not good for my parents' marriage. Dad's photo with Denis Compton as one of the 'Brylcreem Boys' (they looked uncannily alike and were mistaken for each other many times) was all over the London underground during this period. The tours lasted many months, he was now famous in all international cricketing countries, and there were often pretty girls around touring Test teams and BBC commentators.

I think my mother might have been prepared to overlook the unfaithfulnesses. More threatening for the long-term future of the marriage was the fact that he was writing to Valerie. She was seventeen years younger than my father and had been only 18 when she started work as his secretary in 1950. She was painfully shy at first but underneath was an efficient, affectionate, intelligent, generous and humorous personality. She had brown hair and grey eyes, was sturdily built and looked a little like a warmer, more timid version of Angela Rippon, the former TV newscaster.

The relationship developed very slowly and was probably the more dangerous for that – secretaries being in a unique position to know and share affection with their bosses. In fact, the growth from affection to love was so gradual that my father was quite genuinely surprised when he discovered he had fallen in love with her. But that crisis was well in the future, and it was for my mother and us children that he wanted to get home from Australia.

On the outward journey he had found Hong Kong exciting, but Japan was the only country he saw which he wanted to go back to. At heart he preferred the life and sophistication of Europe.

On the return journey he enjoyed the cricket in grass skirts in Fiji; found San Francisco attractive; was unnerved by the hotel doorman in Chicago racing after him to say, 'Don't go that way, sir'; and was impressed by the New York skyline.

When he returned, he found that John Marshall had been pushed out of his job as editor of the *Evening News*. It left a bad taste. My father had no desire to work with the new regime and he had already received an offer from the *News Chronicle*, which was anyway his favourite daily newspaper, so he accepted.

A general election had been called for 26 May 1955 and it was time to fulfil his commitment to stand for the Epping Liberals. He explained why he had decided to stand in his election manifesto:

Dear Voter,
I am not a professional politician. In ordinary times I should be happy enough just to go on earning my living, enjoying my family life with my wife and two sons.
Unfortunately ours are not ordinary times. I am not satisfied that the best that politics and government can mean to us today is sixpence off income tax. I am glad of the reduction but I am worried about issues that seem to me more important. I want my children to grow up in a world which is not at war, not living in the shadow of the hydrogen bomb. I want them to live in a Britain which is not torn by class war – employers on one side, workers on the other – as if the two could not live contentedly together as they must do in any really happy society . . .

To his surprise he enjoyed the campaign. Norman Hoddell, the agent, Howard Davies and other local party members were good company and the gradual climax to election night was exciting.

The Liberals had not contested Epping in 1951. In the election before that the Liberal had lost his deposit, and with the Conservatives in power and the Liberal vote squeezed by a strongly challenging Labour party, saving his deposit was all that my father was aiming for. In 1955 losing the £150 deposit was a real financial penalty for the Liberal party – not the bagatelle it has become now.

He canvassed for only one minute – two doorsteps, to be precise. The first householder said, 'We vote Labour', and shut the door, and the second said, 'What election?' My father could not make small talk or kiss babies; was unexpectedly thin-skinned, and hated the way a householder can treat a canvasser like a travelling salesman, a trade for whom he felt sorry.

Speeches were another matter. He could make those wherever and whenever commanded. He could speak sincerely about politics because his political beliefs ran deep. His speeches had a shape – a beginning, middle and end because they were thought out although they appeared spontaneous. With the experience gained from commentating, he could also alter the content or adapt to circumstances or questions. His mother asked to come up from Basingstoke to accompany him for a couple of nights during the campaign. Television was still in its infancy and campaign speeches were better attended than they are today, though hardly standing-room only. One night my father's morale was boosted when at the end of the meeting an old man stood up in the audience and said, 'I have not been an active Liberal for many years but I like you, young man, and what you have to say, and I will cover your deposit or give the equivalent sum to party funds if you save it.'

His secretary Valerie's parents were Liberal voters as well, so she was more than happy to help. She spent most days of the campaign announcing the Liberal message from the megaphone-betopped van. The late-night bottles of wine the candidate shared with his loyal party workers revived flagging spirits. As she swung relieved into party worker Howard Davies's garage after a long day, there was a loud crash followed by a bouncing metallic clanging. Valerie had forgotten the megaphone, which had struck the garage roof, cleared the low garden wall first bounce and come to rest in the middle of the road.

Graeme Finlay was the Conservative candidate and Leah Manning, later to become Dame Leah Manning, stood for Labour. She had held the seat in 1945, was a former schoolteacher and President of the National Union of Teachers. The campaign was clean. My father saw nothing of Graeme Finlay, who ignored his outrageous challenge to debate the proposition that Conservatism was fundamentally anti-Christ, but he got on well with Leah Manning.

Finlay won with 26,065 votes. Leah Manning was second with 22,542 and my father a long way third with 7,528 votes; but he had easily saved his deposit, the pinnacle of Liberal ambition at the time. At the polling station on election night a dejected Leah Manning turned on my father and said, 'I thought you would take votes from him but in fact you have taken them from me.' My father, who believed that Liberal philosophy is well to the left of centre, could not help feeling sorry for her.

Electioneering was a happy enough experience for my father to repeat in 1959. But when he got more than 15,000 votes, and the first – amazing at the time – Liberal by-election win at Orpington followed in 1963, the prospect occurred that he might get in by mistake. A Liberal MP's wage would not have covered half his financial commitments, so he curtailed his political career, though he always spoke at party rallies whenever asked and was later President of his home Winchester branch of the Liberal party.

My father was writing on soccer as well as wine and cricket for the *News Chronicle*. It was a newspaper he was delighted to work for. It was liberal but less verbose than today's *Guardian*. Although the articles were intelligent, it tried to entertain; and its foreign coverage, with reporters like James Cameron, was unparalleled.

The BBC continued to hire my father for cricket commentaries in the summer and often for 'Any Questions' and 'Guilty Party'. 'Guilty Party' began with the story of a crime. Afterwards members of the panel chose which actors playing in the story they would like to interview. At the end of the programme each panel member tried to guess the criminal, giving the reasons for their choice. It was presented by Ted Mason, who created and wrote *The Archers* and was a close friend. Ted's annual mileage on his frequent trips to London from his home in Birmingham was not far short of my father's around the cricket circuit. One night, returning to Birmingham after a couple of drinks with my father, he was overtaking on the now mainly abolished three-lane stretches of road when a lorry coming the other way also started to overtake. Ted just squeezed back into the nearside lane as it thundered past and wiped the sweat off his brow. It was not until he went to open the driver's door the next day that he noticed the lorry had taken away both offside door handles.

The 1956 Australian tour was the strangest my father had seen. In a wet summer Jim Laker destroyed the Australians on drying wickets to which they were not accustomed. It is sometimes forgotten by cricket lovers that Laker took ten wickets in an innings against them twice that summer – early in the season for Surrey as well as in the fourth Test at Manchester, still known as 'Laker's match'. Tony Lock, who had shared the Australian wickets with Laker all summer, strangely failed to take a wicket in that second innings despite desperate endeavour and with no desire at all to see Laker achieve his record at the expense of his own bowling figures. My father rated Laker the best spin bowler of all time.

During the early 1950s my father's parents would sometimes come up to Highgate Avenue to stay. Jim and I, occasionally just I, would be sent down to Basingstoke to stay with them. Once when I went on my own, my father put me in the guard's van of the Basingstoke train at Waterloo with a label saying 'Basingstoke' around my neck to remind the guard to put me out on the platform where my grandparents were waiting. Like most grandparents they and my father's cousin Molly would spoil us. Nelly would buy us too many cakes and laugh indulgently at our whims.

My grandfather walked slowly with a stick, which was fine for a small boy, and fed me regular butterscotches from his pocket. He showed Jim and me the track from the Basingstoke housing estate where he lived over the wheat-fields to where we could watch the Bournemouth Belle with its brown coaches charge past in a thunderous rhythm of steam and power.

The visits to my parents at Highgate Avenue were a chance for my grandfather to get to the music hall. Nellie was not an enthusiast, so it was a joy for him to take my mother to Finsbury Park or the Metropole in the Edgware Road. My mother found the comedians excruciating, 'but it was grand to see the old boy cackling with joy. He was very generous and would buy me such enormous whiskies I would have to tip some of them on the floor, which was fortunately wooden.'

There is no doubt that my father loved his father but, though he would never have admitted it, he was a little embarrassed about his table manners in the presence of his newfound BBC friends with Oxbridge accents. He also worried that grandfather would tell one too many stories about his wartime experiences in Mesopotamia.

Although my grandfather rarely gave her cause, Nellie could get stern with him if ever she felt he was not behaving correctly. My mother was saddened in one of their last visits to hear her speaking severely to him as he fumbled on the stairs.

'No one gets drunk in Les's house,' she said to him. She still called my father Les, as did most of his family. He was christened Leslie Thomas John Arlott, but from his school-days he preferred, and was called, John or Jack. Perhaps because she was a nurse the moment on the stairs stuck in my mother's brain, for she knew Jack had only had a couple of beers – and indeed the fumbling was the onset of Parkinson's disease, which eventually killed him.

My parents would go down to see him in hospital in Basingstoke. As the tremors increased, he could not handle cutlery. Nellie would bring him sandwiches every day, but near the end he could barely eat them because of the terrible shaking. He died in 1959 in his early seventies, as matters came to a head for my father at home.

Alderney

From the early 1950s we had been taking our holidays in the small, most northerly Channel Island of Alderney. Bill Tayleur, an advertising executive and near-neighbour in Highgate, recommended it to my father and John Betjeman supplied an introduction to one of the island's most eccentric characters, T.H. 'Tim' White, the author of *The Sword in the Stone* and *The Once and Future King*.

The first time they met, my father and Tim were so captivated by each other's company that they went out for a drink and did not return until late the following morning. They did not share a love of cricket. Once, out drinking, Tim knocked his whisky glass off the counter and Dad caught it ankle-high off the ground in the back of his hand. He returned it to the counter without a drop spilt, rather pleased with himself.

'That's the only time I have ever known cricket to be of any use to anybody,' said Tim. Dad thought it an inaccurate observation as it had nothing to do with cricket, simply reactions. When he wrote to Tim one winter asking if he might have his old fishing rods because he was thinking of taking up trout fishing, he touched a richer seam of appreciation. Tim wrote back:

> Dearest John,
> Let me give you bed and breakfast on your way to

Guernsey – but you had better have dinner with your friends at Tommy's as I am still on the water waggon.

Of course you can have the wrecked fishing rods, but I advise you not to. If you are really going to take up trout fishing, which is the most terrific sport in the world, far more difficult in timing than the most perfect on-drive at every cast, far more breath-taking than breaking the sound barrier and far more subtle than Middle Eastern politics, you will not be content with less than the best tools brand new.

I used to be a Big League fisherman, and am the only man I know who once landed a salmon on a trout rod on the mayfly (salmon are said not to feed in rivers) on purpose, and all my bones still ache to do it day and night. I have given it up for moral reasons, one of the great sacrifices of my life, and ought not in theory to encourage you.

I excuse myself by reflecting that I can't stop you, so, if you are going to be a torturer of animals anyway, you may as well be the best kind.

Whales are nothing, coelacanths are nothing, salmons are fools and governed by the laws of chance, coarse fish are mostly worms and bent pins, but the trout, the trout, the chalk stream trout is the emperor of all. You fish for him all day with the cunning of a maniac – which you become – and the skill of a Hobbs or Woolley – glorious, graceful, classical strokes – and the suffocating excitement of dicing with your own death, and at the end of the day you don't know that five minutes have passed. You cannot do this with less than the newest tools and in any case you have to go to a casting school to learn the trick and they are certain to force the purchases on you. Go to the school first explaining that you prefer to let them choose your tackle.

I warn you that if you really take this up you will ruin yourself, as you will have to give up cricket and soccer.

> love from
> Tim

My father did take up fishing later but it never became one of his skills, as you will hear.

'Tim' White looked a bit like Ernest Hemingway – tall, white-bearded and strongly built, also a lover of the outdoors, animals and alcohol, and a writer by trade – but that is where the similarity ends.

In summer he sometimes wore just a large scarlet towelling bathrobe over shorts. One night two rather serious young men came to his door and introduced themselves as Jehovah's Witnesses. Flinging the door open wide, Tim boomed, 'I am Jehovah.'

On another occasion, again in his red dressing gown, he was drinking at a hotel bar in Jersey. The radio was playing loud music which Tim objected to as he thought bars were places for conversation. From his side of the counter he and his companion could see a pretty but rather haughty young woman seated on the edge of the stage across the dining room dance floor evidently waiting for someone. It was about midday. Tim put his drink down and walked erectly across the dance floor to the young lady, who would only have been able to hear the music from the radio faintly. He bowed to her and said, 'May I please have the honour of the next dance?' The young lady dismissed him curtly and without humour, whereupon Tim withdrew still facing her, bowing so that his nose nearly touched the ground every four or five footsteps until he regained the bar.

As we got to know him better and our love of the island grew, we gradually stopped hiring a flat or house and stayed in the cottage adjoining Tim's house in Connaught Square. My mother, Jim and I would fly over as soon as school broke up at the end of July and stay until mid-September, with Dad usually joining us for the last week at the end of the cricket season and any odd days he could get away.

Biographies of Tim White have made him out to be a

melancholic homosexual. I can only say we saw nothing of either. With my mother and us children during those summer holidays he was a riot. He was an enthusiast about movie cameras and making his own films about twenty years before it became popular with the general public – and Tim's films were full of his humour. He would organise imitations of the new 'whiter than white' Persil TV commercials and startle Alderney housewives leaving the grocers by descending on them with a movie camera, my brother Jim as the compere asking which washing powder they had chosen and pulling fresh 'whiter than white' samples out of his pockets like a conjurer if they had not chosen Persil. Even in his early teens Jim could do superb deadpan imitations of smarmy, suave comperes.

On another occasion Tim startled a more staid friend – I believe he was the then Governor of Guernsey – by collecting him from the airport and bringing him straight back to his house as the subject of a simulated 'This is Your Life' programme on the purpose-built stage in the garden. My brother was Eamon Andrews; my mother, made up to the nines, was ushered in as the Governor's forgotten Chinese mistress; and I was his illegitimate son with rice-paddy hat and glued on Chinese moustache. The victim took it in good humour, if a little bemused as Jim presented him with the 'This is Your Life' book at the end, the show's music came up and we all came in to embrace him. There were gales of laughter as we viewed the finished product on Tim's projector the evening after his friend left.

We would swim every day; Ma, perhaps the French au pair (a near middle-aged one with mental problems, my Ma being one for helping lame ducks) or Jim's lady clarinet teacher, Jim and I with Tim's red setter dog, which he was immensely fond of, trampling on everybody in the back. We would set off every morning in Tim's battered old shooting-brake to whichever beach we had decided upon. Usually it was Corblets bay, where there were sometimes

big rollers by the standards of the Atlantic. In many ways
it was strange that my father later decided to retire to
Alderney. He hated beaches and swimming and was never
known to sunbathe in his life – but he did like islands,
especially one where the sea can be seen from practically
all points and where there are tumbling white combs on
the currents that surround the island on even the calmest
days.

After a second summer spent in Tim's cottage my father
was worried that the family was imposing itself on Tim's
hospitality and wrote accordingly. He received the following reply:

> Dearest John,
>   Yes of course I want you next year, though it will
> probably kill me. I am still so desperately lonely for all
> the happiness and rumpus that went on here this
> summer that I have half a mind to go away myself next
> time and leave the house to the Arlotts rather than face
> it again, I mean face the parting.
>   You asked me why I didn't install a mistress. The
> answer is that I don't want a mistress – I want a lot of
> people to hug and feed and worry about and be with. I
> ought to have had a family exactly like yours. But it is
> too late now. I wake up every morning like a creature
> crunching stoically in a trap – no way out. Anyway this
> house is yours next summer.

Tim came to stay with us in London for a week that
Christmas but was usually drunk, which irritated my father
and weakened the friendship. But something else occurred
that summer of 1957 that was to number our Alderney
holidays.

My father liked to hold court at the head of his own
dining table. At home in Highgate, guests were happy to
be entertained or join the entertainment, but in Alderney
everybody was on holiday on a small island and wanted to

get out and about and down to the sea. He preferred to converse over the table at the end of the meal as he did at home, and had no wish to go down to a party like the one everybody was invited to one night on four navy corvettes in the harbour. Leo Harrison, the Hampshire wicket-keeper, and his wife Joan were over with us when the cricket season ended, as was my father's secretary Valerie. Leo was one of the few people outside the family who could take my father on when the arguing got serious, partly because my father knew there was genuine affection and friendship underneath.

My father was extremely intimidating when angry and pushing seriously for his own way rather than arguing over an issue. He was large, had presence, a thunderous black frown and speedy and forceful command of an immediate array of sometimes unscrupulous arguments as to why his wishes should prevail. In later years rows with Leo would be funny again, but at that time I think my mother felt Leo was supporting her.

Ma was on holiday as well, had done the cooking and entertaining and wanted to go to the navy corvettes to the sort of party that was frequently available to my father on the cricket circuit. 'Bugger you, matey,' Leo finished the argument, 'Dawn and I are off down to the harbour.'

My father had discovered almost as a revelation the previous month that he was in love with Valerie. He had found himself obsessed by when she would be coming back from the holiday she had taken to compete in the Torbay – Lisbon yacht race – she was keen on sailing and was the first woman competitor in the race. When he went down to fetch her, he confessed that he was in love with her. She replied without hesitation, 'I've been in love with you for years.'

My father showed the insensitive side of his nature, and perhaps cowardice, in deciding to tell my mother about his relationship with Valerie on Alderney in a house full of holidaying people when she came back from the party on the navy corvettes.

He concluded the conversation (I think my mother was too shocked to make it into a row) by saying, 'Go up and tell her [Valerie] you don't hate her and it's going to be all right.' Needless to say, my mother was unable to do any such thing. Valerie's face puffed up like a balloon in the days of tension before the end of the holiday.

Next morning, Leo's humour and understanding was probably the only thing that helped my mother – hung over after the party and in considerable emotional pain – preserve an air of desperate normality over the mound of washing up and unblinking yellow-eyed mass of frying eggs on the stove for us children and the house full of guests.

I never saw my father cook a meal or do the washing up but he was quite fastidious about other people keeping the place clean. In later years he was a master at carrying a plate dramatically into the kitchen as a signal that someone else should be doing the washing up. When my mother was away once, leaving my father to get Jim and me off to school, he called us half an hour early, inspected us to see if we were dressed correctly, opened the fridge door, gave us a cold sausage each from the plate inside and told us to leave immediately for school or we would be late. It was practically the only time either of us was ever early.

Yet at his own work he was unrelenting. And by the standards of his generation, with his wife a housewife and domestic help several days a week so that she could cope with the near continuous cooking and entertaining, he was not so unusual.

Divorce

'Mummy and Daddy don't want to live together any more, so we'll be living in two different houses,' my 12-year-old brother Jim told me a few months later. He was a good actor and delivered his lines well – with enough portent to convey the finality and importance, but not too emotional – so you would not have known that the night before he had provided my father with one of the most harrowing memories of his life when he clung to him begging him not to go.

'Will you be going with me?' I asked. 'We won't be one in one house and one in another?'

'No, no,' said Jim, 'we'll both be together.' He was six years older than me and had long ago brokered a 'no grassing' pact. He both protected and amused me except when he changed into a character he called 'Manchie' and emerged from the black cupboard in our attic bedroom with a horrific face and terrible voice.

Common wisdom is that children can sense the atmosphere before a divorce, but I can remember neither atmosphere nor rows. It was a large semi-detached house and until Jim's words on the landing as we came down from our bedroom, I had no idea there was anything wrong with my parents' marriage. Dad was away a lot, but things seemed fine when he was home except – from my point of view – at Sunday lunch, when he would invariably banish me into the kitchen to finish my meal because my table manners were so bad. I used to finish lunch on my own in there between sobs. Perhaps because of jumping the gap from working to middle class, good table manners were, he knew, part of being accepted by the new and famous people with whom he was rubbing shoulders.

He only smacked me once. He was trying to sleep early one morning after getting back from Manchester at 2 a.m. and I was lying next to him, prodding and teasing him. He would joke with me when I was older about the terror on my face – not because of the smacking but because he was fully awake, out of bed and had caught me before I could get out of the door and three steps up the well-practised escape route to my bedroom.

Even when he had been away for six months or more on the Australian tour and world tour for the *Evening News*, my father was never a forgotten figure. Large folding postcards would arrive every week or so and Dad would find the right text for a 4-year-old boy. Unfolding snow-covered postcards from wintertime Chicago would have a crocodile, my favourite animal, added somewhere, and he always had something worthwhile to relate, so I knew he was not wasting his time out there.

When I taxed him years afterwards about the divorce, he would be generous – it was his fault, he had been away too much and had not been faithful. He always added that my mother was an excellent mother who had done a grand job bringing us up. At the time, however, he was not so sure about whose fault it was. He sometimes quoted a conversation he had then with Brian Dulanty, an Irish solicitor and close friend of the family.

'You think I'm to blame, don't you?' Dad asked him, sensing criticism in a remark Brian had made. Brian, who had handled numerous divorce cases as a solicitor, replied,

'If you had a microphone in a marriage bed for twenty years you would still only have half the story.'

Coming over from Ireland around the time of the divorce, Ma's Irish cousin Betty Greene went to see my father because she found my mother very unhappy – 'very cheeky considering I didn't really know him,' she told me decades later. To Betty's bemusement (she was a doctor), Dad informed her gravely that the trauma of the whole situation was giving him stomach pains. I used to tell Dad he would die of terminal hypochondria. At one stage at Highgate Avenue he decided he was going blind and bought books on eye exercises, eye washes and eye lotions. He still had good eyesight for an old man some thirty years later.

As I have said, I am sure the marriage could have survived the unfaithfulness, but when my father fell in love with Valerie it cut my mother to the quick – 'the worst pain in the world', as she once described lost love to me.

I may not have heard the rows in a large house, and I have found that friends whose parents are supposedly happily married have far more shocking stories to tell, but there is no such thing as a 'nice divorce'. Of course there were agonies and rows, but their marriage was probably better than that of many who stay together.

My mother said afterwards that she should have been firmer with my father; like many only children he could be demanding, selfish and sometimes almost wilful. In fact, my mother made an amazingly good fist of the enormous change from being married to a provincial policeman to entertaining famous and distinguished people. Had my father's relationship with Valerie been one of those brief but regretted gropes back at youth that men in their forties are prone to try with secretaries half their age, they might have got back together; but his relationship with Valerie was too happy from the outset for that to be considered. My father called the joy of his relationship with Valerie a

'million to one chance', and he was never able to understand how or why it happened.

With the separation, it transpired that Jim was wrong
about the houses – it was two flats we shuffled between.
My father and Valerie took a flat with their office over a
wig shop in George Street off Baker Street, and we moved
to a flat with my mother in Stanhope Road, the Crouch
End side of Highgate. Later Ma began a relationship with
Donald Barrington, an advertising consultant whom she
had met through a mutual friend (Bill Tayleur, the near-
neighbour who had introduced my father to Alderney and
had a house over there). Donald eventually moved into
Stanhope Road.

I missed our large attic playroom in Highgate Avenue,
where my brother and I used to play football with a boxing
glove in a game much like ice hockey as we slid in our
socks at full speed over the lino. In Stanhope Road the
lady downstairs complained when I played football in the
bedroom. A football-obsessed 7-year-old was not the
instant appendage a bookish intellectual like Donald had
in mind when he started courting my mother, but our
relations improved after he had a son of his own – my half-
brother Dominic – some years later.

My stepmother, Valerie, who felt some guilt about the
part she thought she had played in breaking up the family
home, was excellent with children. Weekends in the George
Street flat were contented and relaxed and Valerie was
natural and kind, but she had the good sense never to try
to compete with my mother.

About this time my mother asked to have a meeting with
my father at the Stanhope Road flat. I listened at the door.
I remember the period as the closest to unhappiness in a
happy childhood. Apart from the divorce, I had just moved
to the preparatory school of Highgate School and the
discipline there was harsh after the friendly kindergarten I
had been attending. A third of the pupils were boarders

and at 7 years old they were the most miserable pupils among us. Thus when I heard my Ma suggesting I become a boarder and my father saying he would not have it, I could hardly contain my support for my father and nearly gave away my eavesdropping.

Jim and I would spend the school week at Stanhope Road with my mother and Donald and most weekends with my father and Valerie. Even if he were in the middle of reporting a cricket match in Manchester, Leeds or Nottingham, my father would get back to see us. Fearing that we found the George Street flat a bit dull, he some-times hired a small motorboat and we would chug down the Thames past Execution Wharf and back via the Greenwich shore. We usually had a picnic of salty chicken sandwiches, cold sausages and hard-boiled eggs and Dad and Valerie would share a bottle of Beaujolais. Then back to the flat, where we would play Monopoly. Dad would annoy everyone by ruining the game when he got bored after an hour or so by giving me his sets of houses and Monopoly money and retiring to do some writing.

Divorce was a relatively unusual event in the 1950s and my father was sensitive about people's reactions. New friends, or friends who remained faithful at that time, were prized. He thus felt wounded as well as annoyed when a bizarre occurrence shed an unpleasant light on one of the most regular and liked visitors to the George Street flat. He was a bookseller who had better remain anonymous. Some time later father noticed that a first edition of Dylan Thomas's *Deaths and Entrances* signed 'To John' had gone. As a committed collector of first editions he always looked through book catalogues. Thus it was that twenty-five years later he was shocked to come across a sale listing for a first edition of *Deaths and Entrances* signed 'To John'. He knew at once it was his stolen book and rang the bookseller, who asked him to describe the inscription. My father's memory being what it was, he recalled that the inscription was an inch in from the margin on the blank-paged frontispiece and that the inscription was written in a black ball-point pen.

'You had better have it back, then,' said the bookseller flatly. Under further questioning, he revealed that the book had been bought by a collector in the United States who had recently died and whose affairs had come back on to the market.

My father woke with a start in the middle of that night. He realised it was the long-dead bookseller friend who had stolen it during that period at George Street – and because he knew him, he knew why. It would have been nothing to do with the money but just for the joy of saying to a regular customer and collector, 'I've got that signed first edition of *Deaths and Entrances* you were after to complete your set.' But he remained hurt by the certainty of his detective work.

Valerie was a keen poker player, and an unlikely player who joined their George Street school was Brendan Behan's brother Dominic. He was 'good crack', as the Irish say, but shocked the elderly landlady when he was unable to find the toilet, wandered upstairs and was interrupted by the landlady in the middle of taking a leak in her bath.

It was only through a rare defeat in an internal political battle that my father saw the end of 1958. He had for some time been writing the Friday soccer lead for the *Guardian*. It is the football writer's most dreaded day – too early for the 'sceneset' pieces for Saturday's matches, which appear the following morning, but too late for anything to do with the midweek matches, which have already been reported and chewed over. Thus he asked the Sports Editor, Larry Montague, if he could cover the midweek European Cup match between Red Star and Manchester United in Belgrade.

He was told that he could, but after he had put over his

report on the previous Saturday's match the Sports Editor informed him that the paper's chief soccer correspondent, Donny Davies, would be going instead. My father argued, but was told that if the paper's soccer correspondent wanted to cover the match he would do so.

He was still annoyed as preview pieces reminded him of the match, and on Thursday afternoon he told Valerie, who remained his secretary, that he was going to look at some second-hand bookshops – one of his favourite ways of unwinding. He was in one of them when a lady came out of the back of the shop and said, 'There's a phone call for you, Mr Arlott.'

Only Valerie could have found him. The Manchester United plane had crashed on take-off in snow at Munich on the second leg of the trip home from Belgrade, and they wanted him in the office to write the obituaries of the players and journalists as the names of the dead came through. Donny Davies was one of several journalists who died in the crash.

If it had been a team coach crash on the way to a match in Britain my father would have survived because he was invariably late for football matches. He disliked being in the crush before the start of the game or at the end, so he would invariably arrive about five minutes after the start and leave at least five minutes early.

My brother Jim was a Tottenham fan and would tease Dad about a Tottenham v. Newcastle United match he took him to. It was a 1–1 draw. Newcastle scored through a penalty in the first minute and Tottenham equalised through another penalty in the last. Dad missed both goals, but you would never have guessed from reading his match report, which had a clinical report of both penalties thanks to the agency copy he ripped off the teleprinter on entering the office. He had heard the roar for the goal while he and Jim got into the taxi and had already questioned colleagues closely about who scored the first penalty – which side of the goalkeeper he put it and how it was struck – so he could describe it perfectly.

The Old Sun

The seventeen years my father was married to Valerie were the happiest of his life. On one occasion early in their relationship they stayed at a hotel in the Cotswolds on the way back to London from the cricket. They had dined jovially and well and there were sounds of laughter and delight coming from their room. The walls were not thick and they were interrupted by a thumping and an angry cry of 'Keep the noise down, some people are trying to sleep.' They were taken aback and fell silent when there was a thumping from the other side and a voice shouted, 'Spoil-sport. Anyone as happy as that can make as much noise as they want.' It was a memory my father treasured after Valerie's death.

I do not know why, because we only went there once, but when I look back to see Valerie and Jim together with my father and me it is in a northern French holiday resort like Dinard or Saint Malo in a warm, happy atmosphere. Valerie never fell behind in the wine drinking, and one of her common complaints when there were guests was that my father had cornered all the bottles down his end of the table; yet she never seemed to get drunk. Perhaps the only time was in that brief holiday in northern France. I was already in bed, but Jim, who was wearing a French mariner's beret with a red pom-pom and must have been about 15, asked her with mock seriousness the following morning over the croissants, 'Valerie, why were you standing on the table last night?' (It was a very un-Valerie-like thing to do as she was never exhibitionist.)

'I can't remember why,' she said with a twinkle in her eye, 'but I'm sure there was a very good reason.'

Holidays were often with Leo Harrison at the end of the cricket season at 'Harrison Hall', as Dad jokingly called the large bungalow which Leo and his family, who were builders, built at Mudeford near Christchurch.

My father was very territorial. He usually refused invitations to dine at someone else's house. He preferred his own table where he felt more relaxed. 'Harrison Hall' was an exception. He would have arguments with Leo, often violent ones, but they were arguments rather than rows because they were about a subject (no matter how stupid) and there was a basic affection between them which allowed Leo to let loose. Outside the family, Leo was the only person who could disagree with everything my father said and push him to the limits without being struck off.

One explosively ridiculous row was about the depth of the bar at low tide on the River Avon at Mudeford. My father maintained that it was not over two feet and it was impossible for Leo to take his boat out over it. Many years later Leo confessed he was in the wrong but, like members of the Arlott family, that night he had had enough of Dad laying down the law. 'What rubbish you talk,' Leo countered, 'I've done it several times at low tide and it's at least six feet.'

My father knew he was right and rapidly became furious. They both became so angry that they resolved to settle the matter by driving down to the pub nearest to the Avon. It was closing time, and they reasoned that some of the customers must be anglers and they would ask them as they left what the height of the water was over Mudeford bar at low tide. They agreed they would accept the most common view held by the customers. Fuelled by copious amounts of claret, they were both by now so enraged and frightening that the poor locals meandering out into the car park after a quiet night over a few pints were not prepared for such fury. As they left the bar they were gripped by either Dad or Leo spitting, 'The water over the bar is never more than two feet at low tide, is it?' Or 'The water over the bar is at least six foot at low tide, isn't it?'

Although they questioned all-comers they could not find anyone prepared to disagree with either of them, so the vast sums wagered had to remain in their chequebooks as they returned still arguing to 'Harrison Hall'.

On all matters practical, Leo was the master. He had once reluctantly had to ask permission to enter a house to remove Dad's hook from the sofa where he had vigorously cast it through an open window at 180 degrees to the river bank. Yet despite these ill omens, Leo and Joan agreed to accompany Dad and Valerie on a salmon-fishing holiday to the west coast of Ireland. Leo had persuaded Dad that salmon fishing was his latest enthusiasm, despite a weight of evidence that anything involving such practical skills was likely to escape him. If my father had not become easily bored by lack of progress and Valerie and Joan had not been there to distract them, Leo would undoubtedly have become a proficient salmon fisherman. As it was, the Irish gillies spotted early on that my father was someone who was happier buying them whiskies and supping red wine as he listened to their tips on salmon fishing than actually wading up to his waist in the river waiting for a salmon stupid enough to swallow his guilelessly trailing bait. The gillies would be certain to pass my father's part of the bank frequently during the morning to enquire, 'Is everything all right there, Mr Arlott?'

With their Irish charm, the ladies, Dad and even Leo began to get fonder of the gillies than they were of the prospect of catching salmon despite the exorbitant fee they had paid for their beat on the river. The farewell was riotous. 'You may not have caught many salmon, John' (they were on Christian-name terms long before the end), 'but you have had good crack.' This was Irish overstatement. They had not caught a single salmon in a fortnight, but they had definitely had 'good crack'.

All four were still in uproarious form in Dublin on the way back, where the refined surroundings of the Gresham Hotel did not prevent Leo blandly ordering rice pudding for his dessert. Valerie protested. It was not on the menu, apart from being an extremely downmarket dish to order in the Gresham.

'Any hotel worth its salt will be able to produce rice pudding,' Leo countered. Valerie was having great fun prising ever more vehement justifications from Leo when an unperturbed waiter placed Leo's rice pudding before him.

'There you are,' said Leo, 'what did I say?'

The following summer brought another happy cricket memory. Although nearly 40, Leo was still the Hampshire wicket-keeper and our fortnightly end of season visit to 'Harrison Hall' was brought forward because – for the first time in their history – Hampshire had a real chance of being County champions in 1961.

To avoid the issue going to the last game against their closest rivals Yorkshire, who were a stronger side, Hampshire had to beat Derbyshire at Bournemouth. My father was broadcasting the match; he would have been there even if he had not been. The whole side were his friends – especially Leo and Colin Ingleby-Mackenzie, the Old Etonian captain whose racy declarations and amused rapport with his side had brought them some amazing results and to the brink of the championship.

The match was far from a foregone conclusion. Hampshire made 318 in their first innings, but a century from Derbyshire's South African, Laurie Johnson, and 89 from

Alan Oates gave them first innings lead. Colin declared Hampshire's second innings at 236 for 8, but there was no sign of the pitch deteriorating and Hampshire had less than the last day to get Derbyshire out. Jeremy James, who later became quite a well-known broadcaster himself, was my father's scorer and he gave my brother Jim odds of 5–1 against Hampshire winning. Thinking more with his heart than his head, Jim put a fiver on Hampshire only for Derek Shackleton to produce one of his devastating spells from nothing. Moving the new ball just enough to beat the bat, and devilishly accurate as ever, he removed Johnson and Oates within overs and to the crowd's joy Derbyshire were 24 for 4.

Two more wickets in 'Shack's' second spell ensured that the crowd would have something to celebrate and that Jeremy would lose a lot more than he had earned from being scorer for three days.

My father did not really succeed in his attempts to make the final broadcasts unpartisan, and if one 10-year-old boy was the only sober celebrant with the side in the drinks tent afterwards and at 'Harrison Hall', it is the one game for which I still need no reference book to check the scores.

At the end of the cricket season my father, who always liked to find reasons for emotional decisions, decided to leave London and the flat in George Street for Hampshire. He claimed that the immediate reason was the introduction of parking meters outside his George Street flat, but in truth he had had enough of London. He had been there for nearly twenty years and the city had long since lost the glamour it had held when he was younger. And since he was a freelance, often away reporting cricket or football, he had no need to be based there.

Naturally he gravitated back towards north Hampshire and Basingstoke. The planners had already begun their long-term plan to blow up the centre of Basingstoke, move in 'London overspill', as the relocated unfortunates from the East End were termed, and turn the town into a national guinea-pig; so Basingstoke itself was not considered.

My father and Valerie were looking at villages around Alton when they decided to venture a bit further west. Four miles southwest of Alton, on the A31 at Four Marks, the road drops down a winding hill and the countryside becomes a richer green. My father explained this by saying it is because Four Marks represents the start of a different watershed of chalk soil with the water draining towards the Itchen and Meon rivers. The next small town, a largish village in 1961, is Alresford, which he had occasionally visited in Basingstoke days.

It has a fine main street called Broad Street, although the A31 spoilt the centre of the village in those days before the by-pass. Broad Street used to be two streets until the Irish dragoons, retreating with the Cavalier army after their defeat at the battle of Cheriton, burnt down the middle row of houses. They had orders to torch the whole village, which was considered full of Roundhead sympathisers, but the Roundhead army was hard on their heels and they had to continue fast towards Basingstoke where they made their last stand in the south of England. The locals cleared away what was left of the middle street and renamed the wide avenue that remained Broad Street.

My father admired Broad Street. There was nothing for sale there, but up on the main road an antique shop which had been the Old Sun public house was for sale and my father bought it. The small old saloon bar with the original counter still in place made a snug sitting room and the old billiard room took most of his bookcases and books.

Valerie was heavily pregnant as they moved in, but it was only when she gave birth to a girl who was hastily christened Lynne because she was dangerously underweight that it was discovered that Valerie had chronically high blood pressure. The survival rate of tiny babies in the early 1960s was not as high as today and Lynne only lived a few days. Although Valerie was the daughter and sister of doctors, her blood pressure had never been checked before. The doctors at Winchester's Royal Hants County Hospital told my father that Valerie's hypertension was so severe that she was unlikely to have a normal lifespan. They also told Valerie. With her medical background she immediately understood the implications, but hardly ever mentioned her condition or made any allowances for it.

The only time she did mention it in my presence was when I once volunteered over the dining table that a friend of mine had hypertension and his family were very worried about it. 'Yes,' said Valerie, 'I have it as well.' Like anyone young trying to avoid emotion and unpleasant realities like death, I tried to backtrack, saying I had heard it was more dangerous for a man. Valerie was rarely firm, but she fixed me with a decisive look and said, 'It is just as dangerous for a woman.' Then she changed the subject adroitly – a skill she had had to learn with loud and repetitive male Arlotts over the dining table. My father used to think she was somehow ashamed about having hypertension. I believe that with her innate good manners and unselfishness she thought it was boring to talk about your own health problems.

If he was concentrating on the pain of someone he loved or liked, my father could be as deeply sensitive as he could be insensitive when he was not. He told me once that few people try to hurt; most hurtful remarks and actions are just a result of carelessness. He certainly did everything right in Valerie's eyes after the death of Lynne. Unbidden, for the first time since becoming a freelance journalist he cancelled all engagements and took Valerie to a hotel in West Bay near Bridport. For a week he listened and comforted. He was sad himself but he knew the loss was greater for Valerie, who was terribly keen to have a child of her own.

The joy of country life in the Old Sun after their London flat helped return life to an even keel. Now he had a large house with spare bedrooms and a garden, Jim and I would stay with my father and Valerie for most of our school holidays as well as at weekends. We spent the school week at the house my mother and stepfather Donald had moved into in Muswell Hill.

My father and Valerie bought a big farmhouse table for the dining room and my father began his peculiar existence; only using three rooms in the house when he was not away at the cricket in the summer. When he left the bedroom and bathroom in the morning, he would go downstairs to the room he and Valerie shared as his office, only interrupting his typing of magazine and newspaper articles and books for lunch and dinner in the dining room. No matter that the sitting room was supremely comfortable, he never liked armchairs or sofas and I can only ever see him typing on a hard chair in his office or sitting at the head of the table in a large high-backed wooden chair in the dining room.

He hardly ever watched television – occasionally a European cup tie or a soccer international – but the meals lasted a lot longer than in most English households. It was the style of life he had learnt at Daniel Querre's château near Saint-Emilion, where the long evening meal and conversation with family and guests were the focus of the day – and the Old Sun had a large cellar cut out of the chalk which he filled with wine. There was a trapdoor to another cellar underneath the office which was originally used for hiding contraband (the alleyway 100 yards from the house was called Brandy Mount).

My father had entertained at the head of the table with my mother in Highgate, but now he was established in his fame people came down to Hampshire to see him. He no longer used dinners partly as a means of making new contacts and friends.

The dining table; I will never forget all the hours spent round it or the impressions it made. Neither will my friends who used to come to stay regularly, several of whom have devoted a great amount of time, energy and money in trying to create a household with similar long meals of copious conversation, food and drink.

Valerie was quietly but superbly organised. Like my mother before her, she had to be able to rustle up a three-course meal for six guests who arrived at the last moment as though it had been planned. Luckily she enjoyed company and dinner parties herself and after an hour of preparation was hardly ever away from the dining table.

She sat at the opposite end of the table from my father and would smoke small cigars during the long post-prandial wine and coffee stage. Sometimes Dad would fix on Valerie and tease her at length about having played netball for Kent. 'You realise my wife played for a county,' he would say. 'She was the Kent county shooter, all aggression with her netball skirt jumping up and down over her black stockings.'

This had once embarrassed her but never again. She would sit there exhaling cigar smoke with a humorous wide-mouthed smile. David Rayvern Allen, who has compiled several anthologies of my father's work, once wrote that my father seemed to share an endless private joke with Valerie, but it was one from which the guests were never excluded. Valerie could bring out anyone who was shy or overawed by the vehement arguments over the dining table, but she had little time for anyone who was pompous or conceited.

There was always argument, usually loud argument, but it was rarely personal. It was about a wealth of subjects – the 'English' army at Waterloo was 80 per cent Scottish; Oliver Cromwell's massacres in Ireland were exaggerated; twice as many British visit France as French visit Britain, and so on.

No contender could ever get away with 'I read it somewhere'. My father had three sets of encyclopaedias and a vast array of reference books. When the row was fierce enough, even reference books would be challenged and flung at heads. My father queried, challenged and tackled everything we said, but we had full freedom to do the same with whatever he said, which amazed guests who came from homes where what Dad said went. My father would defend himself forcefully and with a formidable shield or checkable facts, but it was never considered rude to query or disagree so long as you had a cogently argued point to put against his.

Politics and religion, far from being avoided, were particularly prized subjects for gingering up an evening with a dull guest, but certainly from my father and Valerie and sometimes even from us children there was humour, politeness and wit. Guests, especially nervous ones, were given far longer than family or close friends to make their point. People could and did insult each other, but only for not accepting an obvious point which was readily accepted by the majority or laid out in some reference book.

To the family, of course, such combative meals were the norm, but some guests, especially young ones, found it mind-boggling. I remember an early girlfriend of mine coming down from her room still white-faced in the morning, saying, 'Is everything all right?'

'What do you mean?' I said.

'That terrible row you had with your father.'

'What row?'

'About Nelson.'

'Oh, that wasn't a row, that was a discussion.'

If the guest had been a wine merchant, for example, my father might say, 'Did you notice he spoke with real enthusiasm about France and his years there but he never once spoke with any real enthusiasm about wine.'

I would counter, 'He probably thought it was rude to try a sales pitch about his wines in the middle of dinner.'

'No,' Dad would reply, 'I think if somebody is genuinely enthusiastic about a subject they cannot help but bring it up even if it is their livelihood. I don't think he's really interested in wine, it just gives him a chance to go to France often.'

Valerie would chime in on one side or the other and we could continue cheerfully arguing for hours. Her favourite subjects were the sea, Red Indians, education and politics, though she rarely brought them up unless somebody else did. As you can imagine, Red Indians did not come up very often, which was a pity as she was encyclopaedic on the subject. She could list tribes who were only taught to kill by the white settlers. In tribal fights before the white settlers' arrival they were content with a sign of submission from an enemy, like taking a lock of his hair. Valerie explained that this only became the infamous 'scalping' after death when they had to become more vicious to defend themselves against the white man.

She was passionate about education – anti-boarding school and saddened that the comprehensive system was not working as she had hoped – and strongly liberal politically, for the underdog and anti-racist. Above all she was an observant listener and gently humorous. One phrase she liked which probably applied to herself was, 'Before 30 a woman pretends she isn't shocked when she is. After 30 she pretends she is shocked when she isn't.'

My father once wrote to her when away at the cricket: 'Ours has been a marriage such as I used to think could never quite happen. The secret of it is, I fear, that you spoil me so much. But I do try to give something in return – even if it doesn't include washing up. You really are remarkable in remaining mysterious and exciting – someone to be attained – through all familiarity.'

She spoiled everyone. If she saw you liked some dish it

would be on the menu often. If you confessed you could not fold a shirt or make an omelette, Valerie's laughter was gentle as she showed you how. You might find the picture I have painted of her and the terrific happiness of their marriage hard to credit. I can only say that viewing such a marriage up close (I have never seen another one like it) and having Valerie and my mother as the only women I knew properly were probably bad for me. I went to an all-boys school and had only brothers, so for a long time I thought women were basically nicer people than men and did not realise how rare her sort of personality was and how rare such a marriage.

People who are intelligent, humorous, kind and good-tempered can be dull, but Valerie was not dull either. It is hard to bring such a happy household to life. To that remark my father would have quoted Tolstoy: 'All happy families resemble one another, but each unhappy family is unhappy in its own way.'

With reference books prone to fly round the room, more faint-hearted visitors sometimes took a lot of reassuring, but guests like Kingsley Amis used to take our 'cut and thrust' as routinely as we did. Kingsley and his first wife Hilary came to stay soon after we moved to the Old Sun. My friend David Law was staying, and even to two 12-year-old boys who had never heard of him Kingsley and his wife were rewarding visitors. Hilary would sweep past us in the passage palming us three or four multi-coloured cocktail cigarettes from the back of her hand. We would immediately smoke them in the toilet, despite the difficulty of opening the stiff window to let out the smoke.

Kingsley was made for 12-year-olds – not lofty literary discussion but jokes we could understand. When Dad delicately brought up a bottle of old wine from the cellar, Kingsley grabbed the younger one next to it, tasted it with obvious displeasure and said in a crusty old Colonel voice,

With Sir Jack Hobbs, Alf Gover and Leo Harrison at a meeting of The Master's Club

In his pomp

John Arlott, OBE, with Valerie, Robert and Tim in 1969

With Valerie in the early 1970s

Wine connoisseur

Fred Trueman, subject
of an Arlott biography,
at Scarborough, 1962

Basil D'Oliveira
(Worcestershire and
England), Gillette Cup
quarter-final, 1973

In France

Cricket writer, at Alresford

Lunch with cricketing friends. *Left to right:* Patrick Eager, cricket photographer; Ted Dexter; Jim Laker, David Frith, Editor of Wisden; John Arlott, Bob Willis and David Gower

With Pat at the Alderney house

Alderney, 1985

'Butler, have you shaken the port?' Then he would leap to his feet to be the worried butler shaking the bottle ferociously and saying, 'No, sir – but I will.'

The following year we went to stay with Kingsley in Swansea. My brother Jim, apart from doing an excellent imitation of Eamon Andrews in 'This is Your Life', could also do a very good Peter Sellers Indian accent. He gave Dad a burst of it in the car. Dad did not say anything, but after a few miles he stopped the car, gave Kingsley's phone number to Jim, told him to phone Kingsley in the Indian accent, say he was from Bombay University, was a great admirer of *Lucky Jim*, was writing a thesis on modern English writers, and wanted to discuss some of his novel's finer points with him.

Kingsley told Jim that this would sadly not be possible as he had a houseful of guests arriving, but Jim had an answer for this. 'Then, Mr Amis, could I just stand outside your house and admire it?'

'My dear fellow,' said Kingsley, 'I wouldn't dream of it. After coming all this way you must at least come in and have a cup of tea.'

Dad decreed that we must play it deadpan with Kingsley; watch him craning desperately out of the window for his Indian guest and then get Jim to give a burst of his Indian accent several hours later at the end of dinner. However, when Kingsley came racing down the front drive to meet us, saying 'I'm terribly sorry but we've got an Indian student coming to tea and I don't know how we are going to get rid of him,' I was too young to keep it up and spilt the beans.

Kingsley ruminated for a few moments and then said to Jim, 'Come with me.' There was a fellow lecturer at Swansea University, an expert on Dryden whom Kingsley disliked. Jim was to work the same routine on him, but when rejected he was to be more insistent with more stress on the distance travelled. He was also to be sure to mention that he had already discussed *Lucky Jim* with Kingsley Amis. Jim only lasted a couple of minutes with Kingsley's enemy. It was the university vacation, how did he get his home number, etc?

Kingsley had to wait for the following term for the denouement, but it worked exactly as he had hoped.

'By the way, Amis, did you give some ghastly Indian my home phone number?'

'Yes, I'm sorry if it inconvenienced you,' said Kingsley. 'In fact, he was rather a charming fellow, and far from a penniless student, his father is very big in the textile business there. He only stayed a few minutes and he sent me a case of champagne a week later.'

One Thursday in October in the early sixties my father was playing a round of golf with Tony Catt, the Kent wicket-keeper, and Leo on Alresford golf course. Tony, I think, still holds the record for letting through most byes in a day, a harsh statistic because he was suffering from sunstroke at the time. On the way back they noticed a fairground being erected in the Broad Street and decided to go down there afterwards.

They still had a boxing booth at Alresford fair then, and having been a goodish amateur boxer Tony decided to enter. Anyone who could last three rounds with the fairground professional won £5. Knowing that he was going to have an increasing assortment of hopefuls as the evening and alcohol took its toll, the pro soon decided he was not going to exhaust himself trying to get rid of Tony. Usually he administered a couple of hard jabs to the solar plexus – no injuries too bloody to put off the next likely punters, but enough to discourage all but the most determined from wanting to continue. He had difficulty getting to Tony and had to manufacture a clinch before the end of the first round to whisper, 'Take it easy, mate, you'll get your money.'

Although he was in his forties, Leo was still playing for Hampshire, and if Tony was damaging the boxing pro it was nothing to what Leo was doing to the metal pins and the coconut shy. You had to demolish all the pins to win a prize. The bottom ones were heavily weighted but with his classic sideways-on whiplash throw – he was a first-class cover point before he was a wicket-keeper – Leo was causing havoc. His wife Joan was unable to carry all the teddy bears and boxes of chocolate before the stallholder glumly shut down.

When I came down from school the following weekend, there were pet monkeys lining the tops of all the bookcases and it was impossible to get near the fridge for the array of coconuts across the larder floor, and that was just the excess booty left behind. My father drew up a guest list for the following year – nine holes of golf before lunch, nine after, followed by dinner and the fair – and Alresford Fair day came an annual fixture.

The golf competition contestants and their wives would arrive about 10.30 to be greeted by a glass of 'bubbly' and a draw for the prospective winner in which wives and girlfriends would take one of the contestants' names out of the hat.

Dad was capable of causing a stir even before the draw. One regular we shall call Mr Michael had several times come with a different escort although he appeared to be well past the philandering years. Dad decided he had not seen this escort before and, trapped into making an introduction, he put his foot in it.

'And this is John Michael and . . . Mrs Michael.'

All would have been well if he had left it there, but as with all his best faux pas Dad would worry at the problem. He returned to whisper to the woman, 'I hope you don't mind, I thought it was easier to call you Mrs Michael.'

'I *am* Mrs Michael,' she replied. Dad retreated in purple confusion.

Mrs Andrews and Mrs Betteridge, the well-loved local ladies who helped Valerie about the house, a help much needed with my father's continual stream of house guests, laid trestle tables with white table-cloths and flowers down the centre of 'the long room' – the old billiard room when the Old Sun had been a pub. A three-course lunch which lasted several hours would be cleared away and the table relaid for the four-course dinner which came between the end of the golf and the fair.

The golf was of a very low standard and the draw was needed to add some spice to the event. The wife or girlfriend who had drawn the lunchtime leader would ruin the seating arrangements by sitting next to him. They did this to try to protect him from unscrupulous ladies who would encourage him to overimbibe at lunch to give the competitor they had drawn a chance in the afternoon round. Such efforts came to nought, since protection from too much claret from so many directions was nigh imposs-ible, and Leo was the only lunchtime leader who ever made it to victory.

If the standard of golf before lunch was poor, after lunch it degenerated into farce. Leo, whom my father had handi-capped beyond hope after repeated victories (two shots on short holes and three on the long ones), would take his revenge. At the first tee away from the prying eyes of committee members in the clubhouse he would produce an empty Guinness can and suggest that everyone drive off it for the rest of the round. Everyone would make a dog's dinner of this. The ball would fly directly up in the air, coming down a few yards from the tee as the can took the full force of the drive, or scurry into the dense undergrowth around the tee. Leo would tee off last, talking and laughing with everyone else and not looking at the ball as he sent it straight as an arrow 200 yards down the fairway. The generous applause that greeted his first smite would turn to an uneasy silence among the pre-lunch leaders as he repeated the trick hole after hole.

My father's favourite Fair day incident occurred one year when Leo, as ever, was in full cry on the coconut shy and everyone else had stopped throwing to watch. Practically all his throws hit a coconut near the base, though they did not always knock them out. A little old lady, who must have been short-sighted, stepped out from the back of the admiring throng and advanced on the inner circle around Leo. One of the members of this inner circle was the creator and writer of the first twenty years or so of *The Archers*, Ted Mason. Leo and Ted were good friends, but it was hard to imagine two men who looked less alike except that they were roughly the same shortish height. Ted was grey-haired and bearded, stocky, pale, with a paunch and a wide variety of ailments; Leo was fair-haired, tanned, wiry and still a professional sportsman.

'Please, Mister,' said the old lady to Ted, 'could you get a coconut for my grandson?' She thrust just one ball at Ted.

'Certainly, Madam,' said Ted, 'which one do you want?'

She indicated a large one on the left of the shy. Ted, who had a throwing action like a shot putter, turned a bleary eye on the target and propelled the ball upwards in a low, weak arc. It landed low and roundly on the middle of the base – on the only point of the fulcrum where a throw of such little power could have removed such a large coconut. Whenever Dad repeated the story in later years the tears in his eyes would be as much of delight for Ted at his enormous pleasure as he beamingly handed the old lady her coconut as remembrance of the near hysteria of the rude party guests around him.

My father's main claim to fame at the fair was shooting three of the prizes on the rifle range. The plastic gnomes exploded spectacularly. Dad claimed that he thought the gnome prizes were the targets, but he was barred from the stall and the gypsies who ran the fairground speeded up the merry-go-round when he was the sole occupant on the outside horse. He reached a strange angle and friends were aligned to catch him before he entered the saloon bar of the Horse and Groom at 40mph. But generally we were well received at the fair, because, apart from Leo, all attempts to cover the house with coconuts only lined the fairground owners' pockets.

In 1962 Valerie became pregnant again. Once more she had to spend large periods of the pregnancy in hospital because of her high blood pressure. In the Royal Hants she befriended Jill Lentall, who during a hard winter was living in a caravan with several small children. Valerie determined to help. It was characteristic of the happiness of her marriage to my father that they found time to help people. My father pulled all the strings he knew at Winchester Council and many he did not, and Jill was eventually found a council house.

To have the baby, Valerie went to the Hammersmith Hospital in London, which specialised in treating her condition. Although underweight, like his dead sister before him, and delivered by Caesarean section, the baby survived – my half-brother Robert.

Jim

Soon after Valerie and my father moved into the Old Sun in 1961 my brother Jim left school. Like me, Jim was rather more interested in enjoying life than studying for exams. Unlike me, he was in the top stream at Highgate School, then one of the first ten schools in the country for exam results. To his teachers' annoyance and his own disappointment because he had an interview with a Cambridge college before his 'A' levels, his results were not good enough. He could have got into several minor universities, but decided to try to be a newspaper reporter. One of my father's friends, Denis Treseder, was Sports Editor of the *Southern Evening Echo* at Southampton at the time, and with his help my father was able to arrange an interview.

I do not remember Jim being as rebellious as I was six years later about my father organising an interview. I refused to accept his offer when it was my turn, saying I would find a job on my own.

'I can't get you the job, I can only get you an interview,' my father countered. I remained unconvinced.

'Look,' said my father, 'let's say you get yourself an interview for a job as a dustman off your own bat. It's between you and a dustman's son for the job and there is nothing else between you. Who's going to get the job?'

This was harder to refute. 'They have a saying at the

BBC which applies,' my father added. 'Sure, we'll take your brother if he's any good.' This was one of his unscrupulous spur-of-the-moment inventions. I have never heard anyone at the BBC say such a thing.

Jim must have had a bit of a guilty conscience as well because we both did shorthand courses at night school before joining the *Echo*, to help us feel we had worked to get the job.

He got the job, and when I was 12 and still living with my mother and stepfather in north London, Jim went to live with my father and Valerie at the Old Sun. He was very happy there. Valerie was fond of poker and they had regular schools with Jim, my Dad, the Hampshire cricket captain Colin Ingleby-Mackenzie, Leo and Joan Harrison or Valerie's doctor brother Richard and his wife Jenny. It was the only time my father sat in the little sitting room. One night as they counted up the chips in a smoke-filled room and even the losers were too tired to call for another round, Dad pulled back the curtains and opened the window. 'Just look at that moon,' he said. Valerie arrived beside him. 'It's the sun, you fool,' she chortled.

Even after non-poker nights Jim suffered from another family failing – being unable to get up in the morning for the train to work. He had to be at the *Echo* in Southampton some twenty miles away by 9 a.m., which meant catching the little local diesel train at Alresford station at 7.47. Luckily for Jim, by chance two of the railwaymen at Alresford station had sons – Mike Ford and Bob Norris – who were reporters at the *Echo*. Before they would let the little diesel pull out, one of them would run down to where the path across the graveyard joined Station Road. If Jim could be seen, or his long dog strides on the tarmac heard in the distance, they would hold the train. If not, they let it go – but that last chance they always gave him.

Jim was so used to half-mile sprints to catch trains that one night he made an imbecile of himself on the return from

Southampton Central. Observing the Alresford train leaving Platform 3 at speed, he made a last despairing burst over the steps and down the other side, opened the door to the last carriage, and dived apologising onto the startled passengers. He had to apologise more embarrassedly as the train jerked to a halt. It had been on its way into the station.

It was thus with no little joy that Jim said farewell to trains when he managed to persuade Dad to give him an interest-free loan on a second-hand white MG sports car.

I still got on well with Jim, but he did not smile quite so readily at a 12-year-old brother's jokes and was developing a bit of edge. He needed it as a reporter. People still found him gracious and funny, but a reporter's job gets more competitive the better you get and the better the story you are given. He wanted to do well, so in a way more aggression was forced on him. The Beatles were in the ascendant, and when they played at Southampton Jim managed to get into the back of the transport van that took them from the concert. He tried to conduct an interview with John Lennon, but his abiding memory was of Lennon saying repeatedly to the chief 'roadie', 'Where's the fucking bread, man?'

Jim had fewer rows with my father than I did, but he was particularly annoyed about the enormous insurance payments he had to make on his old sports car. My father explained that insurance actuaries were not out to fleece young drivers, they were only really bookies reacting to figures. Those figures showed them that young journalists who were under 25 driving sports cars were particularly likely to have accidents. My father put this forcefully to convey his worry, but Jim felt aggrieved and eventually walked out into the back yard in irritation after they had been over the same ground several times.

It was the last argument they would ever have. To my father's pain, he and the insurance actuaries were right. A week later the 20-year-old journalist in the sports car was dead.

Grief

Jim had delivered one of the chorus girls from a show back to where she was staying in Southampton. My father would theorise that once he was on the dual carriageway at the brow of the hill after passing Winchester around 5 a.m. with just five hilly but straight miles to Alresford, he would have thought, 'That's it, I'm home now' – and dropped off to sleep in that small, warm sports car.

There were no skid marks, so we hope he was still asleep when he went under the solitary lorry ahead of him 200 yards down the straight hill. The lorry had pulled out of a garage at the top of the hill and was still going slowly. Jim's blood alcohol level was below the legal limit, and he could fall asleep anywhere. School friends remembered how the history master had twice insisted the rest of the sixth form move out to their next lesson quietly, leaving Jim to wake up surrounded by giggling third formers who replaced them in the classroom.

Thankfully for his long-term survival, there was nothing British about my father's grief. He continued to work and insisted on covering a football match for the *Observer* the following Saturday despite the protests of his friend, the Sports Editor Clifford Makins. Clifford had not long before lost his own wife from cancer. Knowing the train my father would be on, he went to meet him at Waterloo station, reminding him for the first time through his empathy that he was not the first person to have suffered an unexpected death in the family.

In the days that followed, when my father was not working he was talking about Jim to the family and close friends who came to the house, weeping and losing weight. He would sit at the end of the dining table, his eyes glaring like beacons of pain. Valerie, who was full of sympathy, calmed him and kept him sane. My father would insist we talk about Jim. My friend David Law and I would have finished our meal and would be standing to one side of the table by the mantelpiece. I am sure that if an anthropologist had seen a photograph of the scene he would have said we were subconsciously trying to get out of the line of my father's violent pain and grief. I cried, but I was 14 and 14-year-olds are tough and try to hide from emotions which make them vulnerable.

Dad went round the house collecting Jim's belongings to give them away or burn them. He waded deep into the grief, the only way his personality could handle it. The police gave him back Jim's wallet with a couple of blood-stained pound notes (the policeman had known Jim, so Dad had not needed to identify him). Driving home at night from football matches or engagements in the months following Jim's death, he would charge his car at hapless lorry drivers, swerving away at the last moment. If a lorry driver had not been working on New Year's Eve, Jim would have been alive – so run the irrational thoughts of bereaved parents. The lorry driver concerned had known Jim by sight, had been distressed by the accident and had come to see my father of his own volition.

My father rationalised the pain. The death of a son hurt so much because it was 'against the natural order of things'. Every parent expected to die before his children, and when that did not happen they felt 'cheated'.

Jim's death was on the television news and in all the

national papers with pictures. Letters poured in from all manner of people. Literate friends quoted Thomas Hardy and other writers dear to my father, but the only letter that really reached him was from the younger brother of one of Jim's friends, who wrote that it was always like Christmas when Jim came round because of the laughter and happiness in the house.

Many people, especially parents, can empathise with losing a child, but losing a son of exceptional kindness and charm makes a parent feel that apart from the handful of people who really knew him well no one can believe that a 20-year-old had such memorable qualities. As my father said about him, 'He was the happiest person I knew and just about the best, with my merits and none of my faults.'

When he heard the news the following day, one of Jim's school friends, Alistair Williams, drove round to my mother's house in Muswell Hill in the early evening, parked outside and sat in his Mini throughout a January night refusing my mother's offers to come inside.

No matter how well-meaning, there is often something clichéd or repetitive about people's reactions of sympathy to such a cataclysmic event. One of the few letters my mother kept was in hesitant, laboriously translated English, from a 19-year-old French au pair called Eliane who used to come to the house to see our French au pair. She wrote:

Dear Mrs Barrington,
    For many persons the first day of this year is an entertainment, a day when everybody wants to be cheerful, a prelude to the New Year. I wish you Mrs Barrington and your delicious boys that, but I know for you this day is and will be each year a cursèd day which tears at your heart. I would like you to know dear Mrs Barrington that my heart is near to share your aching sorrow. All my life a picture of James will stay inside me. He was so beautiful with his marvellous blue eyes full of comprehension, so good, so sensible.

The atmosphere at the *Echo* in Southampton the day after Jim's death was an extraordinary one for a large and impersonal newspaper office. Jim had been a leading light in the Benny Green campaign – seeing how many times the fictitious Benny Green could appear in one issue. Before the editor called a halt, Benny was attending the funeral of civic dignitaries in Winchester Cathedral, playing for large numbers of Hampshire non-league football teams, making regular appearances in group photographs and becoming famous as Hampshire's most travelled all-round personality. He had appeared seventeen times in one issue before he was laid to rest.

Jim's friends on the *Echo* set up and contributed to a James Arlott prize for journalism at Highbury Technical College at Portsmouth, the centre for training journalists in the south of England. Presenting the prize there was one of the last things my father gave up through ill health. Nearly ten years after my brother's death, when my father was still in his prime, a former *Southern Evening Echo* Chief Sub Editor, Brian Pook, was making the introductory speech. Instead of coming up with the normal platitudes he said, 'Anyone who knows the Arlotts will know what an extraordinarily close-knit family they are and what an award like this named after his oldest son means to John.' My father, who was emotional and easily moved – particularly after my brother's death – was unable to speak. Someone had to award another prize before he delivered his presentation speech.

My mother did not have the good fortune to be able to grieve like my father. The tears would not come and the pain thus stayed inside longer and perhaps came out in ways she would have preferred it had not. But the pain of the divorce had receded and my brother's death brought my parents together in a way. My father forced himself back into work and refused to cancel a trip to the West Indies with the Cavaliers cricket side six weeks after Jim's death. My mother wrote to ask if being in the West Indies away from the house where Jim had lived had made the pain any lighter.

In reply he wrote:

> No, being in unfamiliar surroundings has not made it any easier. It made it savagely harder: ham-handed though well-meant sympathy almost drove me up the wall and there was no one who matters to me to turn to for comfort: only the empty and bloody hot bedroom. At the moment I am down to underpants and socks with air conditioning on full bore and sweat running down me. But it has toughened me: stopped me crying in public; given me a savage, enthusiastic, atheistic belief. Almost all the time I am not working I think about him. You are right it is the dream – the disbelief – that is killing; you must so far as I can see, for I am a beginner in these matters too – accept, almost hug the fact: never give yourself a moment of cheating: the come-back is too fierce.
>
> It feels to me now that the recurrent shock has almost passed, that there will be a well of sadness in me forever. That will, as I guess, make me a different person, not necessarily wiser or better or crosser or worse but different. Shall hope not to let anyone else suffer from it though.

My father wore a black tie for the rest of his life and never played poker again because he associated it with Jim being at the table. Some friends found these manifestations excessive; perhaps they were. After Jim's death my father would sometimes quote the reaction of Macduff in *Macbeth* when he is told of the murder of his wife and children. The young king Malcolm urges him to 'Dispute it like a man', and swear revenge. Macduff replies, 'I shall do so; but I must also feel it as a man.' My father felt it as a man and, while no one gets over the loss of a child, the fact that he threw himself into the grief made it a purer if more intense pain.

My mother once said with some justification that my father only really came into his own with his children when they could converse in an adult fashion or enjoy the conversation around the dining table. My father had always found time for me but, stung by the snatching away of Jim, he started taking me away for days together on our own. He had a contract with BBC South to write a programme called 'ABC of the South'. The programme was an excellent and cheap way of boosting the regional audience. My father could select any village or town he liked in alphabetical order so long as it was in the BBC South region and write a four or five-minute topographical commentary.

He would research a village, dictate the camera shots to me and type up the commentary afterwards when he was back home. I remember him showing me the hatchway in a pub where Judge Jeffreys had sat during his 'Bloody Assizes', sentencing to death locals who had taken part in the Monmouth Rebellion; the town hall in Newtown, a hamlet in the north of the Isle of Wight, sacked in a French naval raid down the river inlet; and hundreds of other facets of villages and towns throughout the South that his vivid descriptions fixed in my imagination. One March we went to the Isle of Wight to write some scripts on villages my father had chosen. I remember him deciding that we would stay an extra day as we sat in a hired Mini on the Undercliff talking for hours with a thunderstorm buffeting the car, waves breaking on the cliffs below, and finished our cold sausages and scotch eggs while Dad drank claret and black coffee.

In His Pomp

———◆◆———

Jim's death dropped my father into a slough for about a year, but the happiness of his marriage to Valerie, her calmness and the kindness and conviviality of their friends gradually brought back pleasures as the physical pain of grief began to wear off. As a freelance he and Valerie had for many years gone without holidays because he was writing a book or finishing a project. He also refused to take holidays because, despite his successes, he was still unsure of himself, worried that the BBC or another employer might try someone else if he were not around to answer calls. In his fifties, for the first time, he finally had the confidence to take a proper annual holiday rather than a few days here or there.

When he was writing *Fred*, the biography of Fred True-man which he rated the best of his books, there was a Yorkshire phrase he heard which he took to. Discussing what Fred could do when he was at his best, one local cricket enthusiast said, 'Of course that were when 'e were "in his pomp".' My father used 'In his Pomp' as a chapter-heading in the book, and he was 'in his pomp' in his broadcasting and writing career when he was in his fifties at the Old Sun. Years of experience and some acclamation had given him a feeling of trust in his own opinions, and his powers of observation were still sharp.

In *Fred* he described the young Trueman's bowling actions:

> At his fastest, off the long run, he moved up in a curve, swerving slightly out, round the umpire. His coaches had adjusted a few details of his action but fundamentally it was as natural as it was splendid. He stalked back to his mark, arms bowed, at a threateningly muscle-bound gait: but as soon as he gathered himself and began his run he became a different creature. About this time someone described him as a young bull; and there was in his approach that majestic rhythm that emerges as a surprise in the Spanish fighting bull. It steps out of the toril, stands hesitant, cumbersome then, suddenly, sights the peon from the cuadrilla, pulls itself up and sets off towards him in a mounting glory of rhythm, power and majesty. Such was the run up of the young Trueman as, body thrown forward, he moved first at a steady pad and gradually accelerated, hair flopping, and swept into the delivery process. Again the analogy of the bull holds good, for the peak of its charge is controlled violence, precisely applied in a moment of rippling speed. Trueman's body swung round so completely that the batsman saw his left shoulder blade: the broad left foot was, for an infinitesimal period of time, poised to hammer the ground. He was a cocked trigger, left arm pointed high, head steady, eyes glaring at the batsman as that great stride widened: the arm slashed down and as the ball was fired down the pitch, his body was thrown hungrily after it, the right toe raking the ground closely beside the wicket as he swept on. Coming in almost from behind the umpire threw his left shoulder up and helped him to deliver from so near the stumps that sometimes he brushed the umpire. Indeed once, when Sam Pothecary was standing at Taunton, Trueman felled him, as he passed, with a blow of his steel right toe-cap on the ankle so savage as to leave that mildest of umpires limping for a fortnight.

When I was 14, my father started taking me away to the cricket. To watch a whole three-day game, listen to him commentate at Swansea, Worcester, Taunton or Hove and then have the players as guests at the table, was grand for a teenager who loved cricket. South Wales was his favourite cricket destination outside Hampshire because of the string of good friends he found there. After Dylan Thomas and Wilf Wooller there was Cliff Morgan, the rugby international, who became Head of Outside Broadcasts for the BBC (Cliff thought Dad's imitation Welsh accent was the best he had heard from a non-Welshman apart from Peter Sellers); Kingsley Amis, the author; Clem Thomas, another Welsh rugby international and *Observer* rugby correspondent; and Tony Lewis, then captain of Glamorgan but later to play for England and become a fellow commentator. The talk at the table or in the bar with some of the Glamorgan side was never just of cricket. My father liked the dictum, 'What does he of cricket know who only cricket knows?'

He liked cricketers as a breed. He was equally happy to dine with retired cricketers who had been forgotten by all but the most avid fan, or with cricketers who had struck a bad patch or were unlikely to make the grade. He never turned down a request to write an introduction for someone's benefit or retirement brochure, and although he was a freelance throughout that period he never asked for any money for those pieces. It was an affection that was returned, for in 1967 he was asked to be President of the Cricketers' trade union, the Cricketers' Association.

Throughout my school days I would spend one weekend at my mother and stepfather's in London and the other with my father and Valerie in Alresford. I went to school on Saturdays and Dad would usually be covering a London soccer match, so the standing arrangement was that we would meet outside the barrier on Platform 7 at Waterloo for the 1827 Alton train that connected with the Alresford line – or that was the idea. About 40 per cent of the time I would miss it – Dad used to say I caught one in two and I always claimed to miss only one in three. Although he was annoyed, he was more intrigued by this strange personality fault in someone of his own flesh and blood – as his mother had been with his faults. When he had got his breath back after running panting down the platform (only the front four coaches went to Alton), he would ask pleadingly, 'Wouldn't it be less stressful to arrive ten minutes before the train, have a cup of coffee and read the evening sports papers on the platform?'

I never could, but I surprised him one Saturday. There was one nasty ticket collector who would refuse to open the barrier after he had shut it even though the train was still in the station, but the other weekend ticket collector was more generous and I just got into the guard's van as the train pulled out. I knew Dad would have waited by the barrier for me until they shut it, when he would have heaved a deep, resigned sigh and trudged down the platform with his briefcase and portable typewriter to the Alton carriages at the front. It was a long train and only stopped at stations long enough for me to run up a carriage a time, so it was not until Woking, when they uncoupled the back section to go to Havant, that I crashed open the door of his carriage as he was checking Southampton's position in the League tables of the *Evening News* and said, 'Where the hell were you, then?'

His face lit up with his wicked 'old goat' smile. 'You young bugger,' he said. 'All right, then, how did you do that?'

The Alton train also revealed one of my father's weaknesses. He was not arrogant about his position or success, but he had been an only child and expected his wants and needs to be of major importance to others. One autumn night coming back from Waterloo with a bowler-hatted gentleman sitting opposite him in the first-class carriage

Dad pulled the window down because of his love of fresh air and his oncoming smoking-induced bronchitis. The bowler-hatted man shut the window firmly. Dad opened it again and the bowler-hatted man shut it. I am not sure how many times this pantomime went on before Dad remonstrated, 'You can't want to sit here in this hot stuffy carriage with no fresh air.'

The bowler-hatted man found it cold and definitely did. 'What happened next?' Valerie or I asked as my father related the tale over dinner.

'I went and stood in the corridor,' said Dad.

'That must have upset him,' I said, and Valerie and I roared with laughter. My father really thought that despite the row his opponent would come and ask him to sit down. But at least until the very end he could laugh at his faults.

In the late 1960s my father started another annual event. Searching for presents a couple of Saturdays before Christmas in Winchester, he ran short of ideas well before lunch and dropped into the bar of the Eagle at the bottom of Station Hill. Kept by Geoff Rogerson, a congenial landlord from the Black Country, it was the most interesting conversational bar in the town and Dad ran into Alan Charlton, a fellow Liberal from Alresford and art lecturer at Eastleigh Technical College, John Larter, a local potter, and Ray Evans, a painter. The conversation was flowing freely, lunch was approaching and my father asked Geoff if they could take the mixed grill along with extra kidneys, liver, fried eggs and several bottles of Beaujolais in the small room at the back.

Although all were professional talkers – John and Ray were teachers – they were not what you would think of as joke-telling types, but everyone was on song, fired up by the *joie de vivre* of suddenly finding themselves off work, in good company and with time to spare. They were all new to each other's company and at the end of the meal everyone round the table happened to tell a story. It later transpired that the tales told were all favourite stories which had long been burnished to perfection by the teller.

My father told 'The Overton parrot', a folkloric Hampshire story about the White Hart public house in Overton, a village west of Basingstoke. The landlord was a sour character called Halfacre, whose only grip on trade was a talking parrot who in the days long before radio was an essential draw card.

To continue in the Hampshire vernacular as Dad would tell it:

> One day the parrot ups and dies. After two weeks of gazing at a near-empty bar Halfacre goes upstairs; takes out the jar he keeps under the bed; counts out £15 and says to George his assistant barman, 'George, I wants you to go to Lon'n and buy one of them parrots – not any old parrot, mind; not one of them wot ses "Pretty Polly" or any of that sort o' stuff, but one what talks proper like our Peter did. You can go up on yer day off.'
>
> Now George has never been to London before. He cycles in from Overton to Basingstoke and gets on the slow stopper for Waterloo, which finishes Esher, Surbiton, Waterloo. You can see Sandown racetrack from the platform at Esher. All his life George has backed the horses, there is a meeting on and the train seems to be stopped at Esher a terrible time. George reasons with himself that he's got the whole day off; there's a train every hour, so he'll just put a bit of his own money on one race and continue up to Waterloo to buy the parrot.
>
> After the fourth race George has lost all the guvnor's money as well as his own and has only the return ticket to Basingstoke. It's nine o'clock when he gets back to the White Hart, where Halfacre is sitting lugubriously behind an empty counter. He stands up as George enters.
>
> 'Where's the parrot, George?'
>
> 'In a manner of speaking I've got it, guvn'r, and in a manner of speakin' I haven't,' says George.

157

'I don't want no manner of speakin', George, I wants my parrot or I calls for the police.'

'Well, 'tis like this, see, guvn'r. I gets up to Lon'n to this Petty-coat Lane where they's got pet shops from one end of the street to 'tother. I goes in most all of them but none of them has parrots what could talk like our Peter. Most just says "Pretty Polly", that sort o' thing. At last I finds one that talks proper magnificent like, like our Peter.'

'"How much do you want for this un' then?"' I says.'

'"Oh," says the guvn'r, that's the best one I've got, that'll be £20."'

"£20," I says, "you'll find no takers at that price."'

'I stands by the wall at the side of the shop and when he goes out for lunch I follows him down into a little bar – that reminds me, you owes I for the couple of pints I bought 'im over lunch. Anyroad I beats 'im down – £15 he sells it for, guvn'r. I had to come back third-class 'cos of them pints I'd bought. Aw, but proper clever he were for a parrot, guvn'r.'

'"Where are you from, then?" I says as we start off back.'

'"South Amerikay," says this 'ere parrot.'

'"Do you know where you're going, then?" says I.'

'"Nope," says the parrot.'

'"Well, you're going to Overton," says I.'

'"Overton?" says this 'ere parrot. "Ain't there a landlord called Halfacre keeps a pub there that I've heard them talkin' about on the ships?"'

'I wasn't saying nothing, guvn'r.'

'"I've heard all about 'e," says this 'ere parrot. "Of a Sunday afternoon after his old Missus has gone up for a nap, does old Halfacre still lay that red-headed barmaid on the backstairs?"'

'I wasn't having that, guvn'r. I opens the cage, wrings the bugger's neck and throws him out the window.'

'You done right, George, you done right.'

Competition was tough and I do not remember if my father's story won that first year, but it was decided to make the lunch an annual event and that a prize would be awarded by majority vote in following years. Alan Charlton made a piss pot in the pottery; the invitation list grew over the years, and if you drive through Alresford in November you will still find people in bars trying out their entry on any unfortunate fellow customer.

Although best known for his cricket commentaries, my father was a better public speaker. He never used notes, knew what he was going to say before he stood up and would have in mind a clear start, climax and pay-off. He would look at the audience and pick on one receptive person so that he could judge whether he was stimulating, moving or boring.

It was not until I was 16, when I told him that I wanted to get a part in a poetry-reading performance at school, that I began to get an idea of how much thought, preparation and even musical skill went into his public speaking. For years on the 'Book of Verse' he had produced actors reading poetry, plays and extracts from books. Any tricks of the trade he had not picked up he had discovered while teaching at the BBC training school. They were using T. S. Eliot's 'Journey of the Magi' for the school audition. 'Read it to me,' said Dad.

He was not impressed. 'You sound like you are reading the news,' he said, 'and I get the impression that you do not understand the poem. It is a fine poem and if you want to move other people when you read it you will have to be moved by it yourself.'

By the time he had finished, the copy was not only covered with the stress marks which are on most newsreaders' scripts but by pitch marks.

'"Then at dawn we came to a temperate valley" – start that higher and lighter.'

It could have been a piece of music. In fact, when my

father read poetry – which he did on record and on radio – not only did he make sense of the most difficult pieces, his intonation was never regular. He moved the pitch of his voice up and down like a musical instrument.

In the 1960s, Liberal Party headquarters would ask him to speak at any major rally. My father would ask the organiser when he got there whether they wanted a 'rabble-rouser' or a 'tear-jerker'. I was in the audience for one 'tear-jerker' at a rally in London in the late 1960s.

There is no recording of exactly what he said that night. It was several years after the euphoria of the Liberal Party by-election victories at Orpington and other constituencies had faded away. 'People will tell you that the Liberal Party is not doing well in the polls and that a Liberal vote is a wasted vote,' my father said, but he added that in the early 1950s the Liberal vote had been squeezed almost to nothing between the Conservatives and a resurgent Labour Party. Voting Liberal, he said, was not a protest vote or a middle-of-the-road vote: liberalism was generosity to your fellow man, a state of mind, a philosophy to live by, and he explained in simple, powerful terms what that philosophy and that belief meant to him.

He put it more movingly and dramatically than I can remember now. The delivery was slow; perhaps the content was not as remarkable as my emotional recall, and of course the speech was made to a national gathering of the party faithful, but I felt a lump in my throat and tears come to my eyes.

'Well,' I thought, 'it's just because he's my father and I'm empathising with him', but when I turned my head I saw that a lady nearby was crying and someone else between her and the end of the row. It was the musical pitch and the latent emotion in his voice that was more moving than the content.

He was raptly in tune with his audience, and once he saw the slightest fading of attention in the receptive member of the audience he had singled out, he would change pitch or subject – and he never spoke too long.

A rare occasion when Dad could not get a word in at the Old Sun was when most of the 1966 touring West Indian team came to dinner. Wes Hall, the fast bowler, was Dad's favourite West Indian player of that side. Dad thought that, like Brian Statham, who was another fundamentally good person, Wes would have taken many more wickets if he had been a nastier or more ruthless personality. He argued that if Wes had not been such a basically nice fellow he would have bowled bouncers at Brian Close when he walked down the pitch to Wes during his famous century in the Headingley Test match. But it was the topic of spin bowling that dominated the evening. Like all West Indian sides, they were remarkably technical as well as passionate about cricket. When my father remarked that it was well known that wrist spinners spun the ball more than finger spinners, he started a fierce argument from which he was unusually, but definitely, sidelined. Lance Gibbs, as a finger spinner, with enormously long fingers, took the remark as a personal insult and at one stage, with eyes flashing, picked an apple out of the fruit bowl and spun it so hard it made a buzzing sound.

For the family holiday the following spring Dad and Valerie managed to find a cargo boat which took whisky into Bordeaux and claret out. Needless to say, it was a popular boat and it could also accommodate a few passengers. The captain was an unusual character from the East End of London called John Towner. He was a card-carrying Communist. His wife Gianna, who is Italian, was carrying a rifle when he first met her fighting for the partisans near Genoa at the end of the Second World War. He married her and brought her back to Britain, where they had four children around my age. Thanks to the trip both families became close friends, and John and Gianna

eventually moved from the East End of London to Oliver's
Battery near Winchester, where we saw a lot of them.
However, that was long after the trip around several
Bordeaux châteaux which Dad had arranged. Needless to
say, there was a nostalgic stay for Dad with Daniel and
Madame Querre at Château Monbousquet.

The hotel we stayed at in Bordeaux was small and
nondescript and we were all looking forward to getting out
to the châteaux. Daniel had sent a driver to deliver us from
Bordeaux. He was a taciturn fellow who seemed to have
little time for 'les Rosbifs'. Unfortunately, Dad was keen to
practise his French before arrival. When he discovered that
he had left his briefcase and portable typewriter at the
hotel, he tried to say to the driver that he would need to go
back there at some stage to collect them, but his heavy
stress and accent made the driver think this was an
immediate command. As he was already twenty kilometres
out of Bordeaux, the driver did a screeching-tyre 'U' turn,
muttering furious oaths, and to our consternation returned
us to Bordeaux at a rate of knots, dumping us speedily
outside the hotel with Dad's French unable to think of a
way out of the embarrassment. We had a dreary meal in
the hotel. With the vindictiveness of a teenager, although I
had been too shy to try any French myself, I said, 'If you
knew the difference between *revenir* and *retourner* we
wouldn't be spending another night in this bloody hotel.' I
was wrong. It was the emphases in Dad's bad French
which had caused the misunderstanding, but he thought I
was right and chuckled lengthily.

Two days later we had lunch at Château Haut Marbouzet. Unbeknown to us, apart from making very fine
wine, the châtelain was a notorious womaniser known
throughout the Gironde as 'Le Menace'. He propositioned
Valerie when he had sent Robert and I off somewhere and
my Dad had gone to the toilet. This was a smart plan since
there was normally time enough to consummate any act

while Dad was in the toilet, but Valerie amusedly rebuffed Le Menace's advances. He was used to it and continued with the wine that was his second enthusiasm after sex. He brought up two magnums of his award-winning '61 and in a lovingly careful but unfinnicky way after a while checked that they were the exact temperature at which he wished to serve them.

Dad had already told me he would brain me if I continued my adolescent rebellion of drinking beer during this trip, and it was the first glass of wine I really appreciated. Dad went completely overboard. Asked what he thought, two large tears appeared in his eyes, and one trickled down his cheek. This was a matter of appalling Anglo-Saxon embarrassment to a 16-year-old son, but for the châtelain who had made the wine he could have done nothing better. He was immediately out of his chair, embracing Dad while forcing magnums of award-winning '61 into Dad's eager case.

'You appalling ham,' I said as we got into the car to leave, 'how could you cry over a glass of wine?' Dad laughed. 'You may think I'm an emotional idiot but it was lovely, those magnums in the boot will taste superb and we have an open invitation to return whenever we want.'

I could see how my father had been seduced by the life at Château Monbousquet. Daniel Querre was twenty years older, of course, and overweight after too many convivial meals around his own table (as my father was to be), but he was a shrewd patriarchal figure with mischievous eyes and his wife was intelligent, hospitable and smartly turned out in that typically French way.

In the hour before John Towner's ship was due to leave, he and Dad were still discussing where they were going to put all the wine Dad had bought when a shout brought us to the side of the ship. A Citroen with a flat tyre was making a dangerously fast trip along the dockside. A figure leapt hurriedly but unsteadily out. It was Henri du Bosq, 'le Menace'. My father wondered if he had come to make a last desperate plea for Valerie, but it was an ignoble thought; he was carrying a presentation box with a farewell magnum of Château Haut Marbouzet.

That winter, 1968, another tour of South Africa was scheduled. Basil D'Oliveira had long since passed through the Lancashire League into the Worcestershire county side and from 1966 had been a regular member of the England side. Australia toured England in the summer of 1968 and, oddly, after making 87 not out in the last innings of the first Test match, which England lost, Basil was dropped.

Stranger things were happening off the field. South African businessmen, doubtless acting as front men for their government, were desperately trying to find a way their apartheid government would not have to accept an England side which included a Cape Coloured South African. Basil relates in his autobiography, *Time to Declare*, how a top cricket official told him before the second Test match that the South African tour that winter could be saved only if he announced that he would be unavailable for England but would like to play for South Africa. Basil rejected the idea angrily, but after he had been dropped for the second Test against Australia a South African business-man, Tiene Oosthuizen, offered him £4,000 a year for the next ten years with a car, a house and generous expenses if he would leave for South Africa as soon as the English season had ended to be cricket coach and organiser for a body called the South African Foundation.

Basil told him he would not prejudice his chances of being chosen for the tour because he was hoping to win back his place in the England side, but Oosthuizen said, 'If you knew you would not be accepted in South Africa as a member of that tour, would you then take the job?' When Basil said nobody could know at this stage whether he would be accepted, Oosthuizen replied, 'Well, I can.'

When he met Basil a few days later, he said he had it on the highest possible authority that Basil's presence would be an embarrassment to the South African government and Mr Vorster, which meant that it would be better not to go. Basil said he would not change his mind.

The side was announced for the final Test against the Australians and Basil was still left out. As he drove dejectedly back to Worcester, where he was due to play against Yorkshire the following day, he stopped at some traffic lights and saw Fred Trueman, who said, 'What the hell are you doing here, Bas? You should be at the Oval with the England team. Roger Prideaux has pulled out and you've been named. You should be at the Oval, old son.'

Basil could not believe it, so Fred pulled him into a pub to confirm the news. Basil scored 158 and took a crucial wicket in the second Australian innings. He thought he would surely now make the touring party, but when he heard the party announced on the radio in the dressing room at Hove his name was not mentioned. The Worcester captain, Tom Graveney, swore fiercely and, seeing the state Basil was in, took him into the physio's room where Basil wept.

My father was angry. He had helped bring Basil to England and now forces and friends of the very system that had refused to give him a chance because of the colour of his skin were cheating him out of a place in the Test side. However, he knew well that there was no need to spoil the case by getting emotive because the facts spoke for themselves.

Stoked by my father's pieces in the *Guardian*, by other newspaper articles and by politicians, a fire of complaint was raging, and when Tom Cartwright said he was unfit to tour, Basil was chosen to replace him. It did not matter that Basil was now being chosen as an all-rounder when the reason given for his non-selection earlier was that he was being judged purely as a batsman because his bowling was not penetrative enough overseas. South African Prime Minister Vorster said he was not prepared to accept the side and described Basil as 'a political football'. The tour was cancelled. At least the positions were out in the open, my father thought.

Before the South Africans were due in England eighteen months later Peter Hain's 'Stop the South African Tour' campaign was in full swing. The head of Securicor offered his company's services free of charge to keep demonstrators off the pitch. My father told the BBC that he did not want to commentate on the tour and explained why in the *Guardian*:

> For personal reasons I shall not broadcast on the matches of the South African cricket tour of England, arranged for 1970. The BBC has accepted my decision with understanding and an undertaking that my standing with them will not be affected by it.
>
> This course of action has not been dictated by mass influences. Apartheid is detestable to me, and I would always oppose it. On the other hand, I am not satisfied that the tour is the aspect of apartheid which should have been selected as the major target for attack.
>
> It would have seemed to me more justifiable, more tactically simple, and more effective to mount a trade embargo or to picket South Africa House. Surely the Nationalist South African Ambassador is a thousand times more guilty of the inhuman crime of apartheid than Graeme Pollock who, throughout the English summer of 1969, played cricket for the International Cavaliers XI with eight or nine West Indians and before he went home, said: 'What great chaps; there could not have been a better bunch to play with.'
>
> Jack Plimsoll, the manager of this touring team, was an intimate friend of mine on the South African tour of England in 1947, before the election of the first – Malan – Nationalist government, and the introduction of apartheid. Every one of the South African players of my

acquaintance has already played with, and against, non-white cricketers.

Indeed only a multi-racial match, played in South Africa before the Vorster and Verwoerd governments banned such fixtures, provided the expert assessment of Basil D'Oliveira's ability which enabled me to persuade Middleton to give him a contract to play in England. Not all South Africans are pro-apartheid.

Crucially, though, a successful tour would offer comfort and confirmation to a completely evil regime. To my mind, the Cricket Council, acting on behalf of British cricket, has failed fairly to represent those British people – especially cricketers – who genuinely abominate apartheid.

The council might have determined, and been granted, terms which would have demonstrated its declared disapproval of apartheid. It did not do so; nor gave the slightest indication of a will to do so. To persist with the tour seems to me a social, political, and cricketing error. If I were a supporter of apartheid I would feel the same. It seems to me destined to failure on all levels, with the game of cricket the ultimate and inevitable sufferer. If it should 'succeed' to the extent of being completed, what is the outcome to be: a similarly contentious tour four years hence?

It is my limitation (an advantage?) that I can only broadcast as I feel. Commentary on any game depends, in my professional belief, on the ingredient of pleasure; it can only be satisfactorily broadcast in terms of shared enjoyment. This series cannot, to my mind, be enjoyable. There are three justifiable reasons for playing cricket – performance, pleasure and profit – and I do not believe that this tour will produce any of them.

The terms of the BBC charter do not permit expression of editorial opinion. It would not be professional or polite to disagree with my fellow commentators on the significance of the tour within the hearing of listeners. It therefore seems to me unfair, on both sides, for me to broadcast about the tour in a manner uncritical of its major issues, while retaining the right to be critical of them in this newspaper.

My father put the reasons for his refusal to broadcast much more bluntly to Mike Brearley in their conversations for a television series fifteen years later, when he said he would not have wanted his friends to wonder what side he was on.

We got a large postbag after his announcement; most were in favour but some were against. The most unpleasant letter came from the former England cricket captain, Peter May.

In the event, the Labour government cancelled the South African tour because of fears of public disorder. Basil behaved modestly throughout despite enormous pressure from many quarters. He let others take the political sides; he just wanted to play cricket for England, which was the only international side that had accepted him.

My father was invited to a televised debate at the Cambridge Union: 'That politics should not intrude on sporting contacts.' Denis Howell, then Minister of Sport in the Labour government, spoke against the motion, seconded by my father. It must say something about the breadth of my father's friendships that the two speakers 'for' the motion – Ted Dexter and Wilf Wooller – were not just friends but good friends. Both have stayed with the family and certainly harboured no lasting hard feelings over the debate. My father was drinking with Wilf Wooller an hour afterwards, and Ted Dexter told the national press after my father's death, 'He was a great man and he did it all himself.' Here is part of my father's speech:

There is a time in the growth of some political beliefs when they so offend against common morals that they are recognisable as evil and obnoxious to right-thinking people . . . I cannot believe that any gentleman on the other side of the house would happily have played a round of golf with Hitler or Goering, nor I trust do any of them want to make up a football match with the people who directed or carried out the suppression of the Hungarian revolution or who battered down the rise of thought in Dubcek's Czechoslovakia . . .

The clash of political commitment is war, but even this, in present years, is not national, nor racial. The major wars of recent years, those in Korea and Vietnam, have been civil war in which a race has divided against itself on the issue of political commitment . . . But this I believe argues that political commitment is a matter so deep and so profound that when the split is at its deepest then the breaking of sporting contacts is only a trifling casualty. So, Mr President, it would be my wish not only to show that this motion is fallacious but that the reverse, the converse, is a major truth. Mr President, I would go so far, I think, as to argue that political commitment is the only valid reason for breaking sporting contacts.

It is political commitment and political belief that can make a man think that his opponent's views are so obnoxious that he will abstain from playing any game against him as a protest against what that other man believes and also, lest it should be assumed that, by taking part in any activity with the supporters of that view, he gives it his tacit approval.

Any man's political commitment, if it's deep enough, is his personal philosophy and it governs his way of life, it governs his belief and it governs the people with whom he is prepared to mix. Mr President, sir, anyone who cares to support this motion will not exclude politics from sport but will in fact be attempting to exclude sport from life.

Frank Keating of the *Guardian* called it 'a mesmerising denouncement of the resolution'. Ian Wooldridge of the *Daily Mail* said: 'He won the day not only with sane persuasion, but a faultless flow of English so beautiful in

its construction that you could almost hear the commas
and semi-colons fall into place.' But they were both old
friends of my father and probably biased. A news reporter
at the event gave a more objective view:

> In some respects this was a most disappointing evening
> and the proceedings at times did not do justice either to
> their theme or their surroundings. The *pièce de résistance*
> of the evening and the only lasting impression one has of
> it was undoubtedly the deep conviction which permeated
> John Arlott's stirring speech. The only man to eschew
> notes, he thrust his hands deep in his pockets and treated
> the audience to fifteen minutes not only of his inimitable
> and dulcet tones but also of thoughts and beliefs which
> came from the heart and made a deep impression on all
> present.
>
> He surely swayed the voting to his side of the house
> and thus the motion, that political commitment should
> not intrude upon sporting contacts, was defeated by 334
> votes to 160.

It was as the 'D'Oliveira affair' first broke in 1968 that I
left school and my mother and stepfather's house in
London, got a job as a reporter on the *Southern Evening Echo*
and moved down to live with my father and Valerie in
Alresford.

The job was not due to start until the first week of
October and between then and leaving school in July I had
the longest holiday I have ever had. After an unsuccessful
time trying to earn some money playing the banjo in the
Faroe Islands I went to help with the harvest on my
mother's cousin Betty Greene's farm in Ireland. The
holiday was due to end with a fortnight with Dad and
Valerie in Malta, but I had managed to leave my passport
on a ferry in the Faroe Islands before leaving for Ireland.

Increasingly annoyed by my carelessness, my father
tracked down by phone a man who had given me a place

to stay in the Faroes and got him to collect the passport and send it back. By this time my Irish cousins and I had been lent out with the combine harvester and tractors to harvest their cousin Denis Greene's farm. We had just finished harvesting his crop and were in the middle of a rollicking party in Denis's barn-converted flat when there was the sound of a phone ringing.

'It sounds like a phone, Denis,' I shouted as we danced with two girls, 'only you haven't got one.'

'Ach well, there is one here somewhere,' he said. No one in the world could have known at 1 a.m. in the morning that I would be in the middle of an impromptu party in my cousins' cousin's flat, but I followed him out to the open-plan kitchen. Denis got down on his hands and knees and started hurling empty bottles across the floor. The phone, which had been ringing for a couple of minutes, was at the bottom of the pile of bottles. Denis picked it up and said, 'It's for you.' It was his sense of humour to pass along an unwanted girlfriend to some unknown. I was giggling until a deep, angry voice reached my ears: 'Timothy, the next time you leave your passport in the Faroe Islands you can get it back yourself. That poor man has spent the last week getting your passport back from that boat and I think it's damned selfish.'

Of course he was painfully right, although we rowed about it at the time, but later I was incredulous as to how he had tracked me down. Simple: he had got the Irish operator to give him the number of every Greene with an 'e' in County Kildare. He would have telephoned them all one after another asking for me despite the hour, but luckily for the rest of the Greenes in County Kildare the first of the dozen or so was Denis.

This was just the start of Dad's phone-hunting ways. He used to boast that he could find me anywhere in the world within half an hour. Certainly when I went out with a friend or my brother Robert in Alresford or Alderney, there was not a publican in either place who did not receive a call from my father asking him to send us back to dinner immediately. It became a game of cat and mouse. Sometimes we would think we had slipped out and chosen an unlikely pub, only for the publican to tell us before we reached the counter that we were wanted urgently back home. As my father got older and more unscrupulous, dinner would be said to be on the table before it had been put on.

Yet the dinners were worth coming back for. Once it was Neville Cardus, who was the *Guardian* cricket correspondent before my father, remembered with much affection and respect by the previous cricket generation. While he was still a policeman, my father used to buy Neville's books and send them to him to sign.

Neville spoke of his early days in Manchester where his mother was a prostitute. He recalled the first row he could remember when his mother, dressed up to the nines, came elegantly down the stairs. 'You're going out again, are you? You're nothing but a common prostitute,' her mother chided her.

'I,' said Neville's mother, pausing near the top of the stairs and tossing her feather boa further round her neck, 'am a courtesan.'

They then got into lively debate about whether it was more fun writing about cricket and wine as my father did, or cricket and music as Neville had done. Neville finished the dispute. 'Well, I can't speak for you, John, but I'd sooner go to bed with a mezzo-soprano than a wine salesman.'

My father was still collecting books in the 1970s and Bill Fletcher, who kept a second-hand bookshop in an alley off the Charing Cross Road, was another entertaining guest. 'Bill, there must have been a time,' said Dad expansively towards the end of one dinner, 'when – perhaps to complete a not-so-rich customer's collection – you've sold a book at a loss?'

'Never,' said Bill, who then proceeded to tell a tale that my father stole, embellished and retold many times. Bill was going round the second-hand bookshops of Glasgow one cold November day when he found among a few hardbacks in a line of paperbacks a copy of *Croft's Views of the West of England* (now one of the most expensive aquatint books ever produced) with all the lithographic pages intact. It was drizzling and there was only a tatty old plastic awning over the books to keep them dry. He tried to avoid showing any excitement as the owner, a bearded old Glaswegian, glanced at him from time to time. He stuck the book in the middle of several hardbacks, surrounded it with twenty or thirty paperbacks and took them at a relaxed pace to the counter. The owner came over and started totting up the prices: 'Four pence, sixpence, fivepence, one and a penny, one and a penny, ninepence, £540, eightpence, fivepence, one and tuppence.'

'What particularly surprised me,' said Bill, 'was not that the old boy knew exactly what he was doing but that it was exactly the same price I was already thinking of reselling it for in London. I bought it anyway.'

I was learning to drive when I went to live in Alresford. Dad left me to the instructor, rightly reckoning we would be too volatile a mixture if he sought to give me advice. He was thus surprised one evening when he was just about to get out of Valerie's car and I leapt in saying, 'I'll put the car back in the garage. I need some practice starting.'

Dad settled himself back into the passenger seat, folded his hands in his lap and gazed at the garage ten metres ahead. The car stalled once, twice, three times, four times. I rapidly became red in the face with embarrassment and rage, revving the engine fit to bust each time I restarted. Suddenly the clutch accepted my clumsy foot and with a spray of gravel the car shot across the back yard. As we approached the garage door at a terrific speed, Dad said quietly, 'I think we're going to hit the wall.'

I smashed my foot down on the brake. The back wheels slewed sideways on the gravel but somehow just late enough to miss the garage entrance. The front came to rest touching the wall. Dad had put out his hands to stop his head hitting the windscreen. There was a moment's pause. It had been an eventful journey. 'Thanks very much,' said Dad.

Driving was rarely an incident-free operation even when he had learnt to trust me a few years later. I was driving us home down the M3 one black winter's night after he had covered a football match when the car gave a lurch and slowed. I recalled at the same moment that I had forgotten to fill up with petrol after work. This was not an unknown occurrence, and Dad had given me a spare petrol can as part of my Christmas present. His face lit up as we came to rest on the hard shoulder. 'You've got the spare can I gave you.'

'It's empty. I ran out last week.'

'It wouldn't have been worth refilling it?' Dad ventured.

'I didn't have any cheques left.'

He opened his briefcase, balanced a claret glass on the dashboard, filled it from the neatly stoppered bottle of claret within and took a paperback on the Entebbe raid out of the same briefcase. There was a spare glass for any passing AA man as well as me when I got back. The father ready for any eventuality; the son for none.

It was golf that pushed the mutual tolerance beyond the limit. It was fine if Valerie was playing – she would laugh at both of us – but when she was looking after my half-brother Robert we played alone. In a fortnight's holiday at Lyme Regis we never once finished a round together. Dad would begin to take the mickey before a shot had been struck. I would be practising my optimistically violent swing as we waited for the players in front to get out of range. Dad would say, 'Come on, son, off you go; you won't reach them now.'

'Are you crazy? That one I got hold of on Monday would go right through them.'

'What nonsense,' Dad would laugh, 'you won't get within fifty yards of them.'

'I refuse to drive until they've passed that bunker.'

'If you get within fifty yards of them I'll give you a fiver,' Dad would say.

Waiting ostentatiously but fuming until the players in front were out of range, I would top my vicious drive into the undergrowth surrounding the tee. Things would deteriorate over the next couple of holes until I would hurl my bag over the boundary fence, but the instant Dad topped a drive and got stuck cursing in thick rough my drive would go straight down the middle. When he reached my ball an innocent enquiry – 'Is that six or seven you've played?' – would be followed by the singing whoosh of a golf club circling over your head.

Mr Hoare, the golf professional at Lyme Regis, never asked why every day we left the clubhouse together and every day one of us returned half an hour before the other, but we always went back cheerfully next day, hopes undimmed of playing out a completely different scenario.

My father wrote prolifically to keep the exchequer going in the winter. As well as the books, he was a regular contributor to *Hampshire* magazine. Payments were somewhat erratic but Dad greatly enjoyed the comradeship of the editor, Denis Stevens, who used to let him write pretty much what he wanted about the county. Denis also held the Old Sun record for length of meal, which was a difficult trophy to win. I returned from the *Echo* to the Old Sun at 8 p.m. one night to find Dad and Denis still seated over lunch with the cheeseboard and a not inconsiderable number of bottles of claret before them. They invited me to join them and said they had been discussing tricky matters of editorial policy. They were both still highly amusing – perhaps the food soaked up the drink. Denis is a good raconteur from 'Flowery land', the nickname given to the network of streets named after flowers at the north end of Southampton, which Dad knew well from his days on the beat. There was not a break in the conversation as Valerie removed their cheese plates and replaced them with the first course of dinner.

My father reported football matches in the winter but he had been getting increasingly unenthusiastic. He disliked the cynicism of the 'professional foul' – the way a gifted player in full flight with the ball who had beaten another was instantly cut down if he were going for goal. He also missed the chats with the managers on the trains returning home from the games. As the national motorway system was established, the top sides increasingly went by coach and he would not have a Bill Shankly, Billy Nicholson or Stan Cullis to talk to. Some of them would walk down the train looking for him, openly confessing that while they enjoyed their players' abilities there was a limit to how much they could take of their conversation.

My father cherished Jimmy Hill's reply when he said to him once, 'Of course, you were a thinking player, Jimmy.' 'That was just the trouble, John, the others did it instinctively without the pause for thought.' But his favourite soccer observation was Bill Shankly's at a training match. A talented young apprentice professional had just missed scoring from close in against a side containing most of the first-team players and was busy making all kinds of excuses. 'Just stick it in the back, son,' said Shankly, 'we'll discuss your options afterwards.'

It was the fans who really helped my father decide he did not want to report soccer matches any longer – in particular the Manchester United fans, with whom he had two fights on trains when he was in his sixties. A group of them from Leamington Spa, of all unlikely places, got into my father's first-class carriage at Birmingham after a cup tie, chanting and swearing. They were out to provoke. One of them flicked his scarf in my father's face and swore at him when he objected. My father stood up, hit the youth and ran down the train with his briefcase. Happily there was a bottle of claret in the briefcase, so when they came down the train looking for my father, holding the sliding door closed with one hand and the bottle in the other, he said, 'The first one in gets this.'

They spat at him and threw cups of tea over his overcoat, but they did not try to break through. Eventually all but one got out at a station. My father heaved a sigh of relief and sat down, only for the one youth who remained to come into the carriage. Dad stood up again with his bottle. 'So you want trouble, then?'

'No,' said the youth in a strong Midlands accent, 'I've just come in to read me comic.'

My father went on reading his newspaper after eyeing the youth suspiciously, and it was as the train pulled into Leamington Spa some ten minutes later that the youth, who had put on a knuckle-duster, punched him in the face through his newspaper.

My father was looking very lugubrious when I saw him at the Old Sun a couple of days later. His Brezhnevian bushy eyebrows were joined by cut marks from the knuckle-duster and his arm was in a sling.

'It went on for such a long time with no one there to help,' he lamented. 'If only you'd been there.'

'Yes, I wish I'd been there, Dad. What happened to your arm?'

'It's just where I hit the first one,' said my father, fingering tops of knuckles that had gone black with bruising.

'It's a pity that last bugger took you by surprise.'

'Yes,' said my father. 'He didn't get completely away, though.'

'What do you mean?'

'Well, he couldn't open the carriage door and I hit him with the bottle. I didn't get him properly but he landed on the platform on his face.'

'But this isn't so bad, Dad. I can't think why you're so depressed.'

By the following morning my enthusiasm was beginning to get to my father, and when I pointed out that the knuckles on his left hand were beginning to go black, he said, 'Oh, I must have hit him twice.'

About eighteen months later my father had another incident with southern-based Manchester United fans. He returned to his carriage from the toilet to catch two of them stealing his portable typewriter and mac; hit the first one; grabbed the typewriter and mac and ran down the train with the two boys in pursuit. In his escape he met an amateur referee from Hampshire who recognised him and helped keep the youths at bay.

He continued to report football matches for the *Guardian*, but the flashpoint was reached in a row with the Sports Editor John Samuel a couple of weeks before Christmas that year. John was a family friend, but my father was getting harder for any Sports Editor to handle. At 62 he had finally and irrevocably lost his fears of redundancy or of not having enough work and had increasingly decided views about what games he should or should not be covering. John told my father that he wanted him to cover a match at Luton on Boxing Day. Boxing Day was dangerous territory. My father staged a second Christmas Day for me on Boxing Day since I spent Christmas Day with my mother. My father insisted that he had repeatedly asked to have Boxing Day off for family reasons since the start of the season, but John stuck to his guns. Finally Dad announced, 'I can see myself dying of a coronary on the way to the ground at Luton and I am not going to breathe my last in Luton. I am not going.'

After ten minutes John Samuel called back. 'All right, it did not have to be Luton and, if my father insisted, he did not have to cover a game on Boxing Day, though this made it difficult to plan the day's coverage. But Dad had had a Damascus road flash while brooding over the row. 'I'm sorry, John, not only am I not going to Luton on Boxing Day. I am never going to Luton again and I am never going to another football match. I have just realised I don't like football any more and I get no pleasure from going to the matches.'

In fact, he did continue to cover football matches until the end of the season because David Lacey would not otherwise have been able to go on the *Guardian* cricket team's tour of India. But it was my father's last season reporting soccer.

He still enjoyed his cricket, though as with most people the heroes of his youth like Jack Hobbs remained unmatched and the games of his boyhood and his first commentaries were most clearly etched in his mind. He was then the only person in the press box who both wrote a piece for a morning paper and commentated. His writing was at its best in the 1950s, with such articles as his account of meeting Daniel Querre in the Hôtel de Plaisance in Saint-Emilion, but his commentaries improved as he got older. They were probably at their best in the 1960s. In the 1970s they became perhaps too relaxed and self-indulgent, but the cricketing public knew him well enough to be happy to let him get away with it.

Of course, even in his last decade of commentary he had his favourites among the players. The unforgettable Botham Test matches of 1981 were in the year after his retirement, but he had already found him a most exciting player (he used to describe Ian's run-up to bowl as 'like a shire-horse cresting the wind'). Ian was very warm towards my father, and his occasional anti-Establishment stance never worried my father since he was no fan of Lord's himself.

My father's other favourite Test player of his last decade in the game was Mike Brearley. He had from the start recognised a warmth and expertise at dealing with people underneath Mike's more widely acknowledged cool intellect, so he was delighted when his prediction that Botham would come right under Brearley was proved true.

What he had in the last years of his career come to enjoy even more than cricket – and certainly more than soccer – was wine and trips to the wine-growing regions. As wine correspondent of the *Guardian*, he took advantage of an offer to cover the 'Trois Glorieuses', three successive days of feasting and drinking in the Burgundy area in November. Through an intermediary he was put in touch with Christopher Fielden, an Englishman in the wine trade, who lived with his wife Ann in the village of Meloisey in the Burgundy hills above Beaune.

As Christopher recalls their first meeting:

> He arrived from the Rhone convinced he was dying of stomach pains. Ann suggested an 'infusion' of herbal tea. He decided he felt better the next day, asked Ann where she had bought it, went down to the local store and cleared them out of herb tea. At that time I did not know him well enough to know his principle that if two of something do you good then twenty of the same must do you ten times as much good.
>
> He came back for the 'Trois Glorieuses' the following year with Valerie, and when I was lamenting at the end of one dinner that there was not a good book in English about Burgundy, he said, 'Let's write one. I'll find a publisher and we'll write it together.' The result was *Burgundy Vines and Wines*, which was published in 1976.

Christopher was the only friend other than Leo who could get away with sticking Dad back on the right track in no uncertain manner if he was being difficult. Like Leo, he was aggressive enough to try it, and unintimidated, and my father respected him and knew that there was a basic affection which would survive any argument.

A Blow Too Many

———— ◆ ————

In 1974 Visnews, the television news agency I worked for, sent me out to the Sydney office for a year. When my brother Robert wanted to go to Australia some twelve years later my father was clinging and tried to use unscrupulous tactics to keep him from going. In 1974 he still had Valerie and he was at his generous best at a cheerful farewell lunch in the hotel in St John's Wood where he was staying while covering a match at Lord's. He had not enjoyed Australia much, he said, but then he had been married with children. I would be sure to have a good time.

My father's mother Nellie died during that year. She once confided in Dad, 'Life hasn't been much fun since your father died', but in fact for a widow she had had a jollier time than most. My father had bought her a terraced house in Basingstoke and she had two of her younger sisters to live with her after her husband died. The youngest, the permanently cheerful Liz, used to live in the 'Bible Belt' of the American Midwest and would tell you gleefully how her rebellious husband Bill had told the door-to-door religious canvassers of the town that he didn't believe in going to church. The middle sister, Emily, a spinster, was more serious, pro-Establishment, and read the *Daily Express*.

I would have tea with the three of them every evening

when I worked in the *Southern Evening Echo*'s Basingstoke office, and it was the only time in my life I have experienced completely uncritical family support. If I brought a girl-friend round they would later echo one after another, 'We thought she was a really nice girl, Tim, are you thinking of settling down?' Told that the relationship was over, they would wait a decent period of five minutes before Liz would say, 'We thought perhaps she was a bit quiet for you, dear. You're only young once, you get out there and enjoy yourself, Tim', and Nellie and Em would chorus the same sentiments. It never occurred to them that the girl might have left me; obviously, I had decided to move on to play the field.

Em, perhaps because she had had no family of her own, was particularly loyal to the Arlotts. She helped my mother put up the curtains when she was newly wed to my father, and never forgot my, Jimmy or Robert's birthdays, although she was only a great-aunt. Yet she was one of Dad's *bêtes noires*. She never said a word against my father, whom she admired, but Dad maintained that she was 'mean-spirited' in such matters as trying to make Nellie feel guilty when she had an occasional glass of sherry. My father could hardly conceal his amusement when it was the teetotal Em who developed gout. His irrational dislike of her stemmed from some obscure self-pitying incident in his childhood.

My father was a past master at charming other people to do things he was not too keen to do himself. Thus it was typical that though everyone else was encouraged to see Nellie and the great-aunts as often as possible – particularly my stepmother Valerie and myself – my father's own visits were less frequent and of shorter duration. In fairness, that was partly because of his hatred of chatting in sitting rooms, since he was happy enough to talk to them around his own dining table when they came to stay at Alresford.

Nellie was a tolerant woman who was stoic about the

planners' destruction of the town where she had spent most of her life. She would look out of the car window and say, 'Where's Wote Street, son?'

'It's been blown up, Grandma. It's underneath the side of that red-brick shopping mall there.'

'I see,' she would say, without further comment.

Her sense of humour could be deadpan. She took me on a coach trip when I was a small boy to see Salisbury Cathedral. I was startled when the coach went over a large pot-hole with a bang and said, 'What's that, Grandma?'

'We've run over a cow,' said Grandma. Horrified, I demanded to know if it were really so; only then did her eyes crease up with laughter.

She was not truly quiet, but when she did speak it had been considered and passed as worthwhile beforehand. She never prattled or used clichés. She passed on her Liberal views and careful choice of words to her son and was the single most powerful influence on his life.

Nellie and the Aunts had few arguments, considering how fundamentally different their lives had been, though sometimes Emily's *Daily Express* politics irritated Nellie and Liz. Shortly before the end, Nellie came to stay at the Old Sun. She told Dad, 'My brain's going, son, my brain's going. I can't even tell my bloody silly sister Em where she's wrong.' She was 91 when she died, and only in the last few months was the product of that alert, amused and shrewd mind not worth listening to.

My brother's death had already made my father embarrassingly sentimental about his children. My boss in Australia was not impressed by my father signing off several commentaries on Australia's 1975 tour of England with 'and goodbye to our man in Australia'. But the homecoming was fun. Dad insisted I took time off work to go to Essex v. the Australians at Chelmsford, saying he would book the Swan Hotel at Southwold. First we watched Essex spin bowler Robin Hobbs score one of the fastest hundreds of all time. Australia had decided to put the spinners on and wait for a catch, but Hobbs went on and on hitting them over the top and finally made 108 in 46 minutes. It was an exhilaratingly carefree innings to watch and we were in uproarious humour as we drove to Southwold. Dad came into the bathroom in his pyjamas to say he had remembered what he had been trying to remember all evening:

> A Franciscan monk of La Trappe
> Let out a most fearful yap.
> He said 'Pax vobiscum,
> I can't make the piss come,
> I must have a dose of the clap.'

This rejuvenated us both so much that we got dressed and went back down to the bar for another nightcap. I could not get the time off for the other game he invited me to near the end of the season. It seemed we would have many more good times 'away at the cricket' – but disaster was round the corner again.

The last time I saw Valerie before her illness was the following February when she asked me down for a game of poker before her birthday. In retrospect, she made a most uncharacteristic mistake during the game, for she was an excellent poker player, but she was as humorous as ever. The following night we went to her friend Joyce Philpott's house. We knew Joyce and her husband George from the Alresford Liberals. My father rarely felt comfortable in other people's houses, even those of his friends. He much preferred his own table, which was fine for him but tiresome for his wives. George had to drive Dad home when he characteristically decided he wanted to go to bed at 10.30 while everyone else was enjoying themselves. It was a cold night and when Valerie and I left around 1 a.m. her car would not start. I pushed it to the top of a steep cul-de-sac and told her to let it run down the hill. Three times I pushed it back up the steep slope; each time it sped to the bottom, Valerie let the clutch out and nothing happened. The last time it went up someone's garage drive at the bottom of the cul-de-sac. I lay exaggeratedly exhausted across the bonnet and we both laughed till we cried.

A week later my father called me in London to say that Valerie was desperately ill and I must come down to Alresford at once. Since my father could use such odd ploys to get the family together, I found it hard to believe he was not being melodramatic. I recalled an incident a few months before when he croaked at the end of dinner that he did not have long to live and I must pull my chair closer to listen to the details of his will. His face was a horrible grey colour and I was alarmed enough for once to take him seriously. For several years my father had had a deal on 'seconds' Van Heusen shirts, which he used to buy for himself, Robert and me when covering Somerset games at Taunton. It transpired that he had put on one of mine by mistake (they were all the same patterns) and it was one and a half collar sizes smaller than his own. He told me that when he undid the collar that night the colour came flooding back into his face. But about Valerie he was not crying wolf. She had had a brain haemorrhage and her condition was serious.

Visiting someone who has had a brain haemorrhage is a strange experience. The doctors say everyone who has had a haemorrhage remembers exactly what they were doing when the vein breaks because the pain is so intense (Valerie had been helping my brother Robert with his homework). After that it is quite unlike watching anyone die of a debilitating illness. The patient is either unconscious with another 'bleed' or chatting away as normal.

We were going in at different hours to see Valerie. A few days after the original haemorrhage she was in fine form and adamant that my father should not cancel their planned holiday with Terry and Jean Delaney in Greece. With Dad's loathing of heat, Valerie had had twenty years of holidays in temperate climates and this time she had prevailed with her choice of location.

All was well for several days until the next time I came down from London and was first that afternoon to see her, with Valerie's younger brother Richard, who is a doctor. It was one of the nastiest shocks of my life. Richard and I were chatting away as we approached the ward. I noticed that Valerie's bed had been moved and she appeared to be asleep.

'Wake her up,' said the nurse as I hesitated. She did not mention that Valerie's bed had been moved under the sister's eye because she had had another haemorrhage. I shook her gently by the shoulder and she turned unseeing eyes on me, while her hand groped along the bedside table for a bowl of orange pieces which her arm waved drunkenly in my direction. It was at the same time pathetic and frightening. I did not need a doctor to tell me she would die if the haemorrhages continued. In cowardly fashion I tried to get Richard to telephone my father, who was due in a couple of hours, but he countered that my father would be more alarmed if he telephoned when my father knew I was there. I could hear my heart beating as I tried to sound calm on the telephone, but there is no good way to break such news. Richard explained that normally they would operate to close the vein but the haemorrhage was at the top of the spine at the back of her neck and it was too close to the brain to be operated on without a real danger of the blood vessels in the brain going into shock, which results in brain death.

Valerie's condition was like a roller-coaster. She was almost as normal when the bleeding stopped but would drift into unconsciousness when she was having another haemorrhage. As they continued, she stopped mentioning the Greek holiday. She was a little distant, as though she knew she was going away, but she never put any worries or fears on anyone else. She had read that a relatively unknown liberal, Jimmy Carter, was winning Democratic primaries in the United States and she was keen for a real liberal to become President at last. She said how bloody hospitals were, and how when she had been in Hammersmith Hospital for months having Robert there had been a riot in Wormwood Scrubs prison nearby. The prisoners had been banging in unison in their cells and she had felt like joining in.

My father and I decided that the only way emotionally to handle the roller-coaster was to try to convince ourselves inwardly that she was going to die and not to get elated by the increasingly short reprieves.

I was on a work pattern of three 12-hour night shifts at Visnews followed by three days off. The tension in the Old Sun was terrible. My father would be silent most of the time, pacing round odd corners of the house. When he discussed Valerie's condition, it was in grim pessimistic terms which I never tried to contradict.

A week later I was back on day shifts, and in the middle of one of them when Joyce Philpott, who was helping Dad with letters in Valerie's absence to try to keep him sane, telephoned to say that I must come at once because Valerie was dying. I have a strange nonconformist conscience, inherited from my father, about asking for time off and was afraid that a stepmother would not be considered a close enough relation to justify my leaving work. I crashed into editor John Tulloh's office and began to explain, but he is a humane man and he simply took one look at me and said, 'Go for your life.'

My father was at the hospital and I knew that Valerie's son Robert, who was just 13, would be back from school. Should I take him down to Southampton to say goodbye to his mother or would it be too harrowing for him? My mother's house in Richmond was en route to Hampshire, so ironically it was her I asked. I was crying and my mother, who had long put the bitterness of the divorce behind her and was very fond of Valerie, was upset as well. She told me simply to ask Robert whether he wanted to come. Thank God, when I arrived he was not there.

At the hospital the screens were around Valerie's bed. I could see my father's knees under the screen as he knelt by her side. They had a little goodnight routine they used to go through before they went to sleep. He had gone through that and she had responded.

The doctors said she had only a 50-50 chance of getting through the night. When she was still alive at daybreak Robert asked my father, 'Does that mean she has a better than 50-50 chance of getting through tonight?'

'No,' my father said. 'It means she won the first toss of the coin.'

The danger of death was now so great that the doctors decided it was worth the risk of operating. I was at my mother's house in the evening after work when my father phoned to say they had tied up the vein; the bleeding had stopped and the doctors said it had been a success. From his natural pessimism and the lugubrious tone of his voice I could tell he was not convinced. The following day they discovered that the blood vessels in her brain had gone into shock and she was brain-dead, the very thing she had always been terrified of.

Valerie's elder sister Gill and her husband Peter Sleight, who was a heart specialist, were staying at the Old Sun now after cutting short a trip to Australia when they had heard the news. They assured my father that while the hospital staff could not actually kill the patient they would probably 'forget' to give her essential medication.

I could not sleep for fear of the phone ringing during the night to say she was dead, so we asked the night sister to ring us first thing in the morning if that happened. The third morning after the operation that is what she did. It was eight days after Valerie's birthday. She was 44.

For my father it was 1965 again, except that he was eleven years older and there was no Valerie to help him through. Again his instinct was to embrace the fact of Valerie's death so that it could never creep up and surprise him in an unguarded moment. He insisted that I drive him down to the hospital to collect her belongings. He broke down in the ward and again in the car park when he found the last letter he had written her unopened. She had been too ill to know of its existence; he banged his head repeatedly against the roof of the car in his agony.

Mary Samuel, wife of the *Guardian* Sports Editor John Samuel, wrote an obituary of Valerie for the paper:

> Valerie Arlott, who died on the 14th of March, was not the sort of public figure to merit an obituary. As the wife of John Arlott, broadcaster and writer, she worked tirelessly as secretary, friend, critic, wife and mother. To visit their home with its generous hospitality and warm welcome was to view from the inside the workings of a cottage industry.
>
> Valerie was a superb cook but the typewriter was always round the corner and one was often asked to stir the gravy or watch the spuds while an important piece of work was finished. Never without a glass of wine at hand, visitor and friend was left at times to browse among the treasures of the house but the warmth of her personality never left one feeling neglected. I shall always remember the discussion and argument around the table after a memorable meal. Valerie, fierce in argument for the underdog and against social injustices, not always agreeing with John on many matters, but putting her point of view firmly and differing with affection and tolerance.
>
> She devoted every moment of her spare time to her young son Robert, and his interests, and the house was

always open to his friends. He will miss her sorely but
the support of a loving home and family relationship
must stand him in good stead. 'Mum' will be remembered for her love and wisdom, and her legacy to John is
a fine son who will, I am sure, comfort his father in his
grief.

My father had worked Valerie hard, typing innumerable
books and articles and endlessly entertaining, but she
would not have had it any other way.

There was a short service for her at Southampton
Crematorium. I have always found crematoria macabre,
with the terrible rollers for the coffin, the curtains and the
music. I expected a standard 'Ashes to Ashes' liturgy to be
intoned. The priest was old, bald and short with spectacles
and a slight regional accent. He was brief, warm, almost
passionate. His message was that death, especially prema-
ture death, is unbearable but there is life after death. His
small eyes behind his spectacles flashed with conviction.
As we walked out into the car park afterwards Dad said to
me, 'At least he believed it.'

The domestic helps, Myrtle Andrews and Mrs Betteridge, had both been devoted to Valerie. She had driven
Myrtle daily to hospital before her husband died of cancer
and Valerie liked both ladies very much. The only way my
father could keep going was if the routine of the household
continued and there was a semblance of normality –
morning in the study writing, lunch, afternoon and early
evening typing, long dinner and bed. With Robert only 13
and Dad domestically incapable, that meant me cooking
for the dinner parties. My father did not care how many
times worse my cooking was than Valerie's – it was
continuing a routine, something to cling on to.

The former Hampshire cricketer Barry Reed and his
wife Shirley asked us to lunch at their farm near Petersfield
one Sunday shortly after Valerie had died. We were driving

in silence through the empty, green East Hampshire countryside which my father would normally have admired. He told me that personally he could not care if he lived or died but he had to continue for Robert because Valerie had wanted that. He was not being melodramatic or looking for the disagreement that encourages.

Friends and relatives tried to help. Valerie's sister Gill and her husband Peter, who had stayed in the house through Valerie's last weeks, came to lunch with their younger son James. At the dining table I took the mickey out of James mercilessly and he got spectacularly angry. Dad even began to listen and smile at the ease with which James was getting inflamed.

It was a bright early spring day. As we went into the back yard before they went home, James, who was a large youth, tried to take revenge by hurling a frisbee at me. When I gave up he set about doing the same to his father, who had chided him for his ease to anger. I was watching smiling and thought Dad, who was standing next to me, was doing the same when he hissed so forcefully in my ear that it made me jump, 'Fuck it all.' This was not a word he generally used, but it jolted me into immediate realisation of what he was feeling – 'You are still having fun as if everything were the same but it is not the same. My wife is dead and for me nothing will ever be the same.'

He lost weight with the stress but – unlike after Jim's death – nothing seemed to improve. One night when we were dining alone many months afterwards he was more distracted and depressed than usual and left the table early to go to bed. I was worried about him and, after ten minutes or so, decided to go to his bedroom. He did not notice me enter. He was standing fully clothed, shoulders slumped at the bottom of the bed, gripping the wooden bedrail so hard as he looked at the bed that his hands were white. I hugged him. 'Thank you for coming in then,' he said.

Valerie had died in March, and with the cricket season about to start my father got more worried about finding a permanent solution to who would look after Robert when he was away. More selfishly he also worried about who was going to look after a demanding, hopeless man about the house like himself. For a while he got by with a combination of Joyce Philpott and the daily help Margaret Betteridge, but for all their goodwill and love of the family they were both married and could only help temporarily.

At a cricket match that summer a bibulous Pakistani journalist friend took the liberty of saying, 'John, in Pakistan when we lose a wife we marry another.' My father recoiled in horror but the idea stuck. He had heard that Pat Hoare, a secretary he had known at Lord's some twenty-five years before, was still single. One day he made contact and asked her if she wanted to take on him, the household and Robert and act as his secretary with a view to living at the Old Sun and eventually marrying him if she liked it.

The Old Sun was a daunting prospect for a spinster in her late forties. Pat had spent most of her life since Lord's living in flats in European cities as a secretary with the United Nations. If she accepted my father's offer of marriage she would have a large house to run; my father to look after, typing up his work and letters as well as constant cooking and entertaining; a teenage boy to care for and an instant and argumentative family. Nor could things be as before, because Valerie's death had aged my father. Increasingly, he could be morose and difficult. Only the pressing demands of work had brought him back into the world. His rather obsessive and demanding love of Robert and myself must also have made Pat wonder exactly where she fitted in, but she decided to accept and moved in.

Even on their honeymoon in Paris in 1977, Pat only had a few days alone with Dad before Robert and I arrived to join them. The Parisians, who had no idea who my father was, had the measure of him. When he insisted that the main door of the restaurant should be left open because the windows would not go down far enough for his bronchitic chest amid the smoke, the door was speedily slammed shut by another diner.

Pat laughed when years later she saw a repeat of a short TV programme my father had made about Thomas Hardy while Valerie was alive. He described how after the death of Hardy's much loved wife Emma, he had married his second wife Florence as a secretary and housekeeper. Whether it was consciously or subconsciously on his part, she knew that this was the role my father had in mind for her. However businesslike the arrangement was to start with, there is no doubt that he grew to love and rely on Pat in his later years of retirement as he grew increasingly physically and mentally incapacitated.

In the first years after Valerie's death his decline was only obvious to those who knew him well. As the almost physical pain of the grief wore off he began to take part in conversation again, but not as before. Perhaps his strongest point as a cricket commentator was his sharp powers of observation. His ability to listen to and be interested by other people, in tandem with his skills as a raconteur, was what made him a joy to be with at the dinner table.

Before Valerie's death he would listen attentively to any guest, eyes gleaming with concentration and interest, warmly and speedily appreciative if the guest was witty or had a powerful point or belief to express. After her death my father sometimes held forth with the same command, but not only would he give scant attention to anyone who was being less than sparkling, he began to miss moments when guests were witty or stimulating. Sometimes a guest, usually an old friend, would make his eyes light up with interest, but this only made what was missing more poignant.

As Mike Brearley so shrewdly observed in his obituary

of my father in the *Sunday Times*: 'The second loss increased his tendency to lugubriosity. The pleasures of life, of friendship, family, cricket, wine, food, poetry, were real enough, but even the best moments were tinged with an awareness of their eventual ending. So a claret or an innings became "desperately good" and those protruding eyes would fill with tears.'

My father clung on to work as a discipline and enjoyed the company of some of his old friends, but the cricket no longer gave him much pleasure either. The Packer affair erupted the following year. My father was politically involved since he was still President of the Cricketers' Association and sometimes chaired their meetings. An Australian entrepreneur who wanted to 'modernise' cricket, Kerry Packer was not really my father's kind of man. My father personally found three-day English county games the most enjoyable form of cricket; yet he knew well that their financial future was questionable and the one-day game was immensely popular. There was no doubt that Kerry Packer's buying of international cricketers would improve some cricketers' wages, but would it create two tiers – the well-paid Test players and the rest – and cause divisive schisms among professional cricketers? Was Kerry Packer improving cricketers' wages for love of crick-eters or out of pique against the Australian Cricket Board, who had refused to give his Channel-9 TV station exclusive rights to Australian Test matches? Certainly when the affair ended Packer did all he could to make sure cricket officialdom did not mete out reprisals against the players who had signed up to play in his unofficial 'Supertests'. My father had no particular love of the cricket establish-ment, so he was not clearly on either side. In retrospect he found it a dismal and unhealthy two years for the game and was glad when the matter was finally resolved.

There is little doubt that the Test side who suffered most and lost the highest percentage of their players was Australia. The defeats of their official side by England while several of their more talented Packer players had to sit in the wings caused considerable resentment in a cricket and success-obsessed country. I travelled up to Headingley to watch England winning back the Ashes in 1977. Still elated by the win – Dad had always been delighted to see the Australians beaten 'because they take it so badly' – I found Dad in the press box afterwards, but his reaction to a major cricketing event was depressing.

'Tim, why didn't you tell me you were here? I could have given you dinner in the hotel.' But the tone was more accusatory than friendly. He got the wine glasses out of his briefcase and we had a glass of claret, but there was no sense of celebration; no question of inviting favourite players or fellow journalists out to dinner, as he would have done before. There was nothing he wanted to say about the day's play. He was fretting over whether he would get back to Alresford before midnight, the kind of anxiety he would increasingly display in the years to come.

He was still popular in the cricket press box, but whereas he had always been charming and modest to admirers who interrupted him, he now started to become dismissive. Once a pleasant young journalist came up to him and said, 'You won't remember me, Mr Arlott, but I used to phone your copy for you when I worked for Hayter's in Brighton.'

Of old, my father would have feigned remembrance, interrupted him with a disarming smile and said, 'So you worked for Reg, did you, what was that like?' Now he let him finish his embarrassed speech, gave a vague smile of acknowledgment and turned to speak to someone else with an 'Excuse me.'

I was angry when I first saw the change. 'Dad,' I would hiss, 'that's no way to treat someone who's come up to say something pleasant to you.'

'Well, why does he have to interrupt me when I'm writing my piece?' he would complain, but it was not the interruption that bothered him. The grief, and the detachment it gave him from what was going on around him, made my father sometimes unpleasant and self-absorbed as he had not been before. Perhaps someone who no longer really cares about life or the future still cares about his own basic needs but no longer much cares whether he is loved or appreciated, especially by strangers.

He also got more cantankerous on air. One of his particular dislikes was presenters of sports programmes who ask the reporter at the ground for all the details of the score, give the details themselves from the studio, and then hand over to the reporter. An unfortunate presenter tried this on Dad. 'And now we go over to Taunton where Graham Burgess reached his half-century a short while ago and Somerset have just taken first innings lead. Is that right, John Arlott?'

'Yes,' said Dad. There was a long pause as the anchorman gradually realised there really was not going to be any more. 'And now on to Bristol to see how Gloucestershire are getting on against Leicestershire . . .'

In the press box he typed his piece for the *Guardian* at the end of play. For years he had carried two bottles of wine in his despatch case and a few glasses for whoever he might talk to. The depth of his colleagues' affection was shown by the obituaries they wrote after he died. Even I was embarrassed by how glowing some of them were, but most of these colleagues had been his friends as well as admirers of his work.

Brian Johnston volunteered self-critically that my father was disapproving of the 'cakes' and 'Johnners' banter. Trevor Bailey in the *Observer* recalled Dad's timing when commentating on a Gillette Cup final: '"Van der Bijl is coming on to bowl looking like a taller, stronger, healthier version of [pause] – Lord Longford." Then came the second pause and with perfect timing he rounded it off with "but not nearly so tolerant."' Or Ian Wooldridge: 'He had the generosity of many men whose talent is so exceptional that rat races do not exist. He would berate shoddy politicians, crooked statesmen of any hue and rudeness, which he abhorred. But never once did I hear him denigrate a colleague or rival less gifted than himself.'

Big decisions at home were usually taken in the manner of the film *The Godfather*, though thankfully they concerned less sinister matters. Although he hardly ever went to the cinema, I insisted that Dad should see *The Godfather* and *Bonnie and Clyde*. He hated them both and walked out before the end. He thought they were very realistic but perhaps they reminded him of his police days, for he loathed the way a nobody could become a somebody once he has a dangerous weapon in his hand. Many scenes in *The Godfather* struck a chord with me because in the film major decisions were taken at all-male meetings. All Dad's children were male, and it seemed to me that big decisions in our family were taken in the same way, although Valerie was always there during their marriage. My father was also emotional and affectionate but concise and decisive in the style of Marlon Brando's 'Godfather'.

As soon as we were old enough to sit round a dining table and take part we would be called in to talk over any of my father's most important decisions, like refusing to commentate on the South African tour; retirement; moving house; his will. Such decisions were discussed round the table with Jim, briefly with Jim and myself, and then with Robert and myself. He listened carefully to what we had to say and sometimes, as we grew older, would take the most flattering course of all – modifying a decision or changing it altogether according to what we had to say.

About the retirement we were all in agreement. Even before Valerie's death my father had been planning to retire at about 65. He said he wanted to go while people still asked 'Why?' We agreed. And though he did not stick to this decision so well, he decided that there would be no farewell performances. Dad used to tell the story of the legendary Spanish bullfighter Manolete, who was gored to death making one farewell performance too many, and we wanted people to remember him at his best. He still liked cricket, but he was tired. For many years he had been the only person in the press box who both commentated and wrote a match report for a newspaper. The increased travel, now that there were so many one-day games around the counties, was not the fun it once had been, especially as many of his friends on the cricket circuit had died.

The long standing ovation from crowd and players after his final commentary during the England v. Australian Centenary Test match in 1980 moved the family. I never heard my father mention it, but I am sure he had given a lot of thought to finishing with just the usual handover to the next commentator to avoid sounding sentimental or self-indulgent – traits he was unfortunately unable to avoid when he was later tempted to make more 'final' broadcasts.

After the first few months of retirement he began to get unmanageably difficult on occasions. We were already worried about how he would perform when he was asked to present the TV Sports Personality of the Year award just after Christmas. My palms were sweating as he was announced to make the presentation speech; as usual it was live and he worked without notes. His speech struck a sombre note on what was meant to be a celebratory evening, but I wager most people who watched the programme remembered my father's speech long after they had forgotten which sportsmen won the awards. The Welsh boxer Johnny Owen had died after a world title fight in the United States that year, and after referring to this and saying that perhaps Johnny Owen should have got the award, he said the British should sometimes ask themselves whether they take sport too seriously and life not seriously enough.

As Pat slowly stopped wrestling with an immovable object like my father and began to realise that his sons could be allies against his more ridiculous and demanding excesses, she found her own niche. Alresford was difficult, though. Pat found and cultivated her own friends, but for many people Mrs Arlott would always be Valerie and Valerie was a hard act to follow. However, after a return visit out of the blue one February it was my father more than Pat who first became keen on the idea of retiring to Alderney, where we had holidayed regularly until some twenty years before.

That February, Alderney was springlike and ten degrees warmer than the British mainland. We were staying in the Georgian Hotel. Pat had realised by this time that the best plan was 'If you can't beat 'em, join 'em', and we had a high-decibel family argument in the restaurant on the first night. The first was about the size of the Alderney population, Pat and I on one side and Dad and Robert on the other. 'You fool, there weren't even 5,000 people on the island in Victorian days when all the now derelict forts were manned by hundreds of soldiers each,' Dad thundered.

Old ladies were leaving their meals to get away from the noise, but the head waiter, Andrew Montgomery, was the sort of man who would have given Dad and Leo a blunt answer during the legendary row over the depth of the River Avon. When Dad asked him in a voice thick with menace how many people there were on the island, he answered smoothly, 'The wintertime population is 1,800. There are about double that number during the holiday season.'

An answer that covered all aspects of the dispute spoilt the battle, so we changed teams – Robert and Pat against Dad and I – and moved on to how many cars there were on the island.

'Be sensible, how can there be as many cars as there are

people?' The restaurant was now empty, but the bar customers were getting restless. Andrew, who had heard the argument from the back of the kitchen, returned to collect the coffee cups and volunteered before he was asked that there were between 1,000 and 1,250 vehicles on the island. He accepted Dad's offer to join us for a digestif and everyone decided they liked Alderney.

Decline and the Fall

Some friends blamed Alderney for my father's decline. They say he would not have gone so steeply downhill if Alderney's inaccessibility had not deterred the fleet of friends and acquaintances who would have been popping in had he stayed on the mainland. I do not agree. The main factors that brought him down, apart from Valerie's death, were retirement itself – stopping broadcasting was traumatic for a virtual workaholic – and the deterioration in his health from chronic bronchitis, cancer, one – possibly two – heart attacks and, most importantly, two strokes.

When the day arrived to put his signature on the dotted line for 'The Vines', as he renamed the Alderney house, my father came out in a nervous rash and was unable to sign. His old schoolfriend Jack Donovan would not have been surprised, with his observation that underneath a bombastic nature my father was quite highly strung. It was not buying 'The Vines' that made him anxious so much as the knowledge that he was signing away the Old Sun where he had spent the twenty happiest years of his life and where his wife and eldest son had lived until they died. If the Alderney estate agent, polite but exasperated, had not pointed out that under Alderney law my father was already liable to pay 10 per cent of the price if he did not sign, he might never have done so.

In fact my father found good friends on Alderney, though he would have been surprised in earlier days to think that his best friend in retirement, Geoff Rennard, would be a Yorkshireman and former Conservative party agent. In the first years of his retirement his new-found Alderney friends were quite diverting enough for Dad – André d'Aquino, a Pole who made statuettes of famous cricketers in his pottery, and Jim Morgan, a retired farmer who turned an inhospitable hillside into a market garden, caught and smoked fish and flew planes, among other hobbies. It was more my father who let his friends down through failing health.

As life expectancy increases, to watch a loved parent becoming old and decrepit is something more and more people are having to endure. The trouble is that while medical science can increasingly extend life, it cannot yet maintain its quality. With your own parents it is a downward path you observe with chillingly detailed memory, aware that it may mirror your own.

The most dramatic deterioration before my father's stroke came in his first year of retirement. In cricket, 1981 was a particularly painful first season for him to miss. He admitted that he would have loved to commentate on the legendary Headingley Test match against the Australians which Ian Botham turned round. He found it almost unbearable to be just another spectator.

My wife Tricia and I were living in Tokyo that year and had long been looking forward to my father's visit, but it left me shocked and worried. Dad excelled himself, demanding wine in Japanese restaurants where we had already repeatedly told him there would only be beer or saké. He was asked to address the English-speaking reporters at the Tokyo press club, and I was depressed to hear him almost taking praise for granted when throughout his working life he had been modest and sincerely thanked anybody who complimented him.

Then, to remind me of times past, there would be a touch of the old charm. The day before he was due to leave he was more relaxed and I was able to play him a record by the Cotswold poet Frank Mansell that I hoped he would like. Normally, if he wanted to converse and the record-player or the TV was on, Dad would growl, 'Switch that thing off, would you,' but the three of us listened rapt to poems about cricket and the blackthorn in wintertime Gloucestershire as four lanes of traffic roared past below in humid summertime Tokyo.

When we returned to Britain in 1983, we found that, progressively, when my father went out for a family dinner the evening became a trial. If we went to Alderney for a long weekend, with Robert, we would spend the first couple of nights round the dining table at 'The Vines'. Then I would say, 'Let's try the new Italian restaurant.' There would be enthusiastic agreement from all, except Dad.

'I'd so much sooner stay here. We've got food in the larder, wine in the cellar.'

'But you're not doing the cooking or the washing up,' we would answer.

So, perhaps with a rearguard plea to go instead to the familiar 'First and Last' restaurant where they put up with my father's many wants and smiled charmingly, Dad would go along to the new Italian restaurant. On arrival, Dad would ask, to the waiter's incredulity since it was March and there was a gale blowing outside, 'Do you have anywhere cool?' We would be given a table by a door or an open window.

We would be chattering away waiting to be served but Dad would already appear detached, taking deep ostentatious breaths. 'Christ, it's hot in here,' he would say.

'Try and think about something else,' would be the stock reply to this opening gambit, but everyone knew what the next move would be. After about ten seconds Dad, who had no intention of thinking about anything else, would call, 'Waiter, could I have a glass of dry white wine and could you get that window over there open?'

The couple sitting underneath the window would look pointedly out into the March gale or show more positive signs of disagreement. If the waiter were versatile or had few enough customers, rather than responding, 'That window doesn't open', he would say something like, 'Maybe I could put you over here and open the door into the back garden.'

If he won some minor victory like this and everyone had to get up and move, Dad would beam, thank the waiter courteously and might sit through the rest of the meal, though he would be urging everyone to 'chase it up' long before the end. If he was told that the window did not open, a favourite rejoinder was, 'Well, there must be some way to get some air in here, I'm perspiring with the heat.' He would rub his red and white-spotted handkerchief over his forehead to demonstrate.

'I'm sorry, sir, but we are trying to keep the place warm for the rest of our customers.' By now the crisis would have stopped us talking and made Dad's temperature the only matter of import.

'I'm sorry, but aren't you hot, Tim?' he would ask.

'I'm not hot, Dad. Perhaps if you lost some weight you might get cooler.' I knew what was soon going to happen and was anxious to reach the denouement. We would order our food, then resume talking but in less relaxed fashion. Suddenly Dad would stand up dramatically. 'I don't think we're going to get any damn food. I'm going to sit in the car to get some fresh air.'

If we pleaded and said we had only just ordered, he might wait a few minutes or even a whole course before repeating the act; but in later years, as we all became resigned to the script, no one would try to stop him going out to the car.

In his first years on Alderney he would start honking the

car horn if left outside for more than a few minutes. As he got older he would just sit in the front passenger seat, demonstrating that it really was a matter of the heat, smoke and stuffiness aggravating his bronchitic chest and overweight condition as much as the selfish, bloody-minded part of his character.

After he had ruined everyone's evening, if we all left early he might be quite happy to have a glass of wine round his own dining table when we got home. In his last years he would go straight to bed, with Pat's help. Robert, my wife Tricia and I, who would normally not have seen him for just about long enough to have forgotten that this was sure to happen if we went out to dinner, would then discuss the decline in his health and personality in dismal terms, until Tricia would say, 'If we discuss the decline in your father's health in this room any more I'm going to go mad.'

His last radio broadcast which reached any semblance of his old standards was made in 1984 when 'Any Questions' came to Alderney. He irritated Labour MP Ian Mikardo with his views of modern trade unionists: 'I've been a trade unionist all my life – my father and grandfather under threat of the sack founded the NALGO branch in Basingstoke – I'm no anti-trade unionist. But the fact is, you see, the trades union movement has become sloppy. People like Ernest Bevin and Aneurin Bevan would have been picked up by the modern educational system, they'd have gone to university, they would have become university dons, they'd never have been in the trades union movement at all. Now the modern educational system scoops up all those with good brains and takes them away and it leaves those who can't pass their "O" levels to be trades union leaders. If your intellect is thus limited and you have a chip on your shoulder you're not an ideal leader of working people.'

For one programme he could still lift himself, but Robert

and I were alarmed when he agreed to do a series of conversational programmes for television with Mike Brearley. Mike was a friend and handled my father sensitively, but those who had not seen him for a while were shocked by his frail appearance. He was self-pitying and over-emotional to an extent which would have made him blench a few years before and which he had managed to avoid altogether during his final radio commentaries.

The *Guardian*'s Sports Editor, John Samuel, provided him with the sort of journalism suited to his retirement years when he asked my father to pick and write about his desert island cricket team. They decided that it did not mean the strongest or the finest eleven but the one he would most enjoy watching. I don't think many of his selections would surprise. His side was Jack Hobbs (Surrey and England), Wilfred Rhodes (Yorkshire and England), Vivian Richards (Antigua, Somerset and West Indies), George Brown (Hampshire and England), Keith Miller (New South Wales and Australia), Ted Dexter (Sussex and England), Mike Brearley (Middlesex and England), Ian Botham (Somerset and England), Learie Constantine (Nelson, Trinidad and West Indies), Jim Laker (Surrey and England), Doug Wright (Kent and England), Wesley Hall (Barbados and West Indies).

Perhaps the only surprise is that he left out Frank Tyson and Leo Harrison – but he included them in the Alderney side his eleven would play against, on the grounds that they had both played for Alderney when he brought them over in the 1950s. On that occasion one of the Alderney side was disappointed to hear that Frank Tyson did not intend to bowl at the equivalent of a village-strength Alderney side on the island's bumpy matting wicket. When Tyson got to hear of this, he asked people to clear the pitch, ran up and bowled one ball at full speed. It pitched two-thirds of the way down the wicket and hit the sight-screen on the boundary without bouncing.

There were some good moments in the retirement years, though they were few and far between. One morning my father stopped our constitutional drive around the island by commanding me to pull into the 'First and Last' restaurant at Braye Bay. It was barely 11.30 and the proprietress, Rita, a favourite with my father, was preparing for lunch. By the time I had deposited Dad, who walked with difficulty, and parked the car, he had ordered a dozen oysters each and a bottle of Chablis. We were the only customers at that hour; the windows were open; we looked at the sea sparkling in the early spring sunshine and nattered happily. That morning he had the holiday spirit that the best of retirement can bring.

He was still capable of raising a smile. He invited a touring team of Australian Aboriginals who played a game on Alderney to come to the house for drinks. Dad was asked to say a few words and remarked, 'When I first saw them with their green caps and insignia, I thought they could have been the Australian touring team if it weren't for their perfect manners.'

Since before Valerie's death, every time I visited my father for annual festivities he had said, 'I don't expect I shall live to see the next Christmas, Fair Day or birthday.' In 1985 his hypochondria turned into reality when his Alderney doctor, Struan Robertson, diagnosed cancer of the bowel, which was confirmed by further checks on the mainland.

My father's brother-in-law, Peter Sleight, recommended a surgeon at the Radcliffe hospital in Oxford, where he worked. We were warned that because of his chronic bronchitis an operation could be dangerous, but now that there was something genuinely and seriously wrong with him Dad became quite courageous. Robert, Pat and I were at his bedside the night before the operation. He said a farewell, 'in case', in an unmelodramatic way and sent me out to buy a bottle of Fleurie. The moment it was finished, he dismissed us with an immediate and satisfied goodnight. We were tearful and tense as we left, but there were no complications during the operation and alert eyes met ours over the newspaper the next evening. 'Have you got that Gravadlax and Chablis I asked for?' he said, giving us one of his wickedest smiles.

There was another highpoint in his retirement. His new Yorkshire friend, Geoff Rennard, drove Dad down to Saint-Emilion where, with many others, my father received some local tippling award. There was a large group of farmers from Lincolnshire there and, to the bemusement of the French to whom he was just another English wine tippler, there was a resounding crescendo of applause when Dad received his stripes. It was so loud and went on so long that the locals, after a few whispered questions about this man 'Elliot?', thought they ought to join in themselves. This Englishman, they thought, had at least had the sense to sink a few bottles of Saint-Emilion in his time. Dad gave a deep bow and returned highly amused to his table.

Another trip to Cherbourg with my father was not so amusing for Pat. He was in his fretting mood and discovered that he did not have a French plug for the nebuliser machine he used several times a day to ease his bronchitis. He demanded immediate action. It was Sunday evening and far from an emergency, but in the end the receptionist called the fire brigade. Such evenings with my father were only amusing in retrospect.

One spring weekend in 1986, when we had a house full of guests, the first really debilitating blow struck. My father telephoned in an agitated state. He could not organise his words, but he wanted me to come at once. He had had a stroke. The basic faculties returned, but more subtle aspects of the brain were lost – he was never able again to dial a telephone number with ease and he retreated further into a demanding, obsessive world of worrying about his health.

A few months later he had to make a rare trip to the mainland so that the doctors could check whether there were any signs of secondary cancers. I drove him to Oxford and Pat, Robert, Trish and I waited in a restaurant near the hospital. On his return, he reported in a flat voice that the doctors had said there were no secondary cancers, but he added more animatedly that they had said his chest was worse. I wish there had been no element of truth in our joking that he seemed disappointed not to have been told the end was near.

Peter Sleight, who had organised the check-up, had not seen my father for about a year. He was shocked by the depressed way he ate his meal, his head down, hardly saying anything. He phoned later to say that my father's doctor should be asked about anti-depressants, but Dad was already on a cocktail of drugs for his many ailments.

I had one of the last meaningful conversations with him the following summer. He said he wanted me to drive him down in the car to watch the Alderney single-wicket cricket competition. It was more to get out of the house than to see the cricket. The single-wicket competition was a knock-out event, the winner being the one who could score most runs off two overs of a competitor's bowling. By gritting my teeth I managed to hit the last ball of a better player's couple of overs for four and reached the final. It was Alderney's festival week and more people than were watching wanted us off the Butes cricket pitch for another event. I was bowled second ball, needing two runs for victory, by a 16-year-old.

Dad slouched silent in the passenger seat. He did not want to get out and have a drink with the players as he used to, and I started to drive him home. His decline was such that I did not think he had been taking the cricket in, so was surprised when he said, 'You didn't think winning that competition was very important, did you?' I knew he thought many people took sport too seriously, but he had always been something of a winner himself. It occurred to me that I might have disappointed him a little by not trying to win when a little cup and a kiss from the Alderney carnival queen were a shot away, so I paused before replying, 'Not really, Dad.'

'You're right,' he said, 'it doesn't matter a damn.'

January 1987 brought a severe freeze to the British mainland and broke all records on Alderney, which was even colder. It snowed, all the palm trees died, pipes froze; my father's house was flooded and he and Pat moved into a guest-house. Thankfully, there was a diversion to dilute Dad's worries and dislike of being away from home. Just hours before the cold belt settled, a pair of secret lovers had arrived in Alderney from Guernsey for an 'away day'. Their plan was to return to Guernsey on the last plane with their spouses none the wiser, but because of the freeze there were no planes for five days. First they had to explain to their respective spouses that they were on Alderney and would not be home that night. Then, as the truth slowly dawned to the spouses left on Guernsey, the soap opera got more dramatic. The pair received increasingly fierce phone calls from Guernsey. Dad observed them closely but discreetly, phoned me with frequent bulletins, and reflected that there were worse dilemmas than frozen pipes and flooded houses.

That same month our son Lucas was born, my father's first grandchild. Dad was above all a family man. Had he been younger, he would have been overjoyed. As it was, he smiled at the baby and hugged him but was often abstracted. Nevertheless, I will remember the first time Lucas made my father laugh.

My father's only exercise now consisted of 'taking a look at France to make sure it's still there'. For most of the year this meant putting on his coat, taking his stick, crossing the road in front of the house, up some steps, fifty yards across the allotments on the other side, then another fifty yards to the brow of the slight rise from where there was a clear view of France.

One cool April day my old friend David Law came over to Alderney. He had been staying in the house when Jim was killed in the car smash many years before and Dad was fond of him. We resolved to take Dad over on the new French boat to Pascal's restaurant at Goury on the rocky Cap de la Hague. We sensed that it might be his last visit to France and he did too, though nothing was said. As we approached Goury on the restless waves of the Cap, the polite French crew began eyeing Dad, worrying how they would get his large and unsteady frame up the sheer ladder on the quay. I saw their looks and said, 'Don't worry, he's prehensile like a cat, he'll be up there in no time.'

They looked amazed until David laughed. In the end we lowered Dad down the side of their boat into a rowing boat and thence ashore. Pascal slowly grilled a large fresh fish after giving us several aperitifs, and we were all very hungry by the time he brought it to the table. Lucas had just moved on to solids; his head swivelled round 360 degrees and he spoke for us all when he uttered a long, low 'Cooor' as Pascal approached the table. Dad took great delight in his grandson's relish of his first French meal, and when Lucas fell asleep over his third piece of lamb, Dad helped lower him into his basket under the table. We finished the last bottle of claret in the hour before the boat returned, in the warmth from the open fire. Dad's relaxed state recalled better times. It was a fitting farewell to France.

My father could not now walk more than a few yards because of his bronchitis and generally poor condition. He started a ritual whereby Robert or I, or a friend if we were not there, drove him round the island every afternoon. His favourite stop was a lay-by at Clonque Bay on the north-west of the island, looking over the dangerous waters of the Swinge to the Casquets light. One afternoon Robert and he had only been there a few seconds when a car containing three youths swung in and parked beside them. One youth was cleaning his fingernails ostentatiously with a knife, and they were all jeering and making faces at my father. Robert took this for about a minute and then got out and told them to 'Bugger off'. His car door, which he opened in rage, hit theirs. He then got back in the car and drove off. He was just nearing the house when the youths' car came from the opposite direction, turned round and gave chase. When Robert stopped and got out, two of the youths ran at him. One jumped on his back while the other punched him with a fist wrapped in a studded belt, lacerating his face – until people playing on the golf course, who had seen what was going on, ran up and intervened.

My father appeared on Channel Television that night looking old, confused and distressed, and reports appeared in most national newspapers. The youths were charged with assault and possession of a knife and my brother with damaging their car door. A reporter from the *Guardian* wrote an interesting piece before the court case suggesting that the island was divided over the incident and that my brother, who is admittedly large, was a public-school 'rugger bugger' type. This was certainly a strange theory to us since everyone on the island who had mentioned the incident expressed sympathy for Robert, including the father of one of the two youths involved, who called to apologise. The youth's solicitor had evidently taken the *Guardian* piece to heart which gave rise to a cross-examination of Robert that he and I later enjoyed.

'May I ask what school you went to, Mr Arlott?'

'Montgomery of Alamein.'

'Is that a public school?'

'No, it's a secondary modern.'

'Do they play rugby there?'

'Yes.'

'Did you play rugby?'

'Not much, I wasn't very good at rugby.'

'Which sports were you good at?'

'None, really. I was quite good at swimming, I suppose.'

The Alderney Jurat, as the island's magistrates are called, cleared my brother of damaging the youth's car door but to our amazement also cleared them of assault, though one of them was found guilty of possessing a knife.

My father used to joke that he wanted to die falling down the cellar steps, and in January 1990 he almost did. He had nearly reached the top of the stairs with half a dozen bottles in a basket when he fell backwards. He knocked himself out, broke several ribs, lost a lot of blood and was covered in bruises; and he would have choked on his own blood and vomit if John Gatrell, a friend who was visiting, had not heard a noise and gone to investigate. In the local hospital he was making little progress, so Pat and Robert had him flown to Southampton General Hospital. He had also contracted a chest infection. Graham Stirling, my father's chest doctor, was on his morning round of the ward when he suddenly realised that he could not hear my father's distinctive wheezy breathing coming through the open door of his room. He was choking and had stopped breathing. Graham brought him back to life and phoned me in Paris to go over right away as it could happen again. It did happen again the following morning, but again Graham was on hand to bring my father round. After an appalling flight in a near-hurricane which closed Southampton airport, I reached the hospital that evening.

My father looked yellow-faced and he was still covered in bruises from his fall. I knelt by his bed and cried. 'Dad, I only hope my son will be half as proud of me as I am of you. I'm sorry I've been such a bugger to you these last few years but it's been hard watching you fall to pieces.'

He smiled. 'What do you think it's been like for me?'

Even then he had a trick up his sleeve. That evening,

when Graham went in to see him, my father made much play on Pat, Robert and myself leaving the room so that he could speak to Graham alone. Robert and I dropped Pat off at a hotel in Southampton to be near my father and we drove down to Leo Harrison's house at Mudeford. We were halfway there when I suddenly realised what my father had said to Graham Stirling. He had asked that if he stopped breathing again the next morning they were to let him go. We drove up to the hospital early next morning and I taxed Graham with it. He acknowledged that that was what my father had said but added, 'We are not in the killing business here.'

My father was moved into the Intensive Care ward to be kept under still closer observation. Ever since I could remember my father had never eaten dessert, except perhaps a mince pie at Christmas. In the Intensive Care ward I saw him being fed hospital jelly and ice cream and he appeared to relish it. It was the ultimate point of depression for me. I could not work out why it was so important to me at the time, but I think it was an irreversible sign that the fight and personality were sliding out of him.

The chest infection went. The bruises from the fall slowly disappeared, though he walked with great difficulty afterwards, usually with a frame, and with a wheelchair for emergencies. If he was difficult and demanding before, he became even worse now that he was hardly able to walk. He was endlessly restless or ill at ease. He had a bell with which he called Pat and June, the nurse who came most mornings, for any minor thing that occurred to him. He phoned friends asking them to visit him because he was frightened of being alone, and when they arrived he was generally too depressed and obsessed with his health to speak to them.

Ian Botham flew himself over to visit Dad once when he was visiting Jersey, and he took a fancy to Alderney. He rented a house, and he and his wife Kathy and Kathy's

parents Gerry and Jan Waller would call in several times
when they were staying on the island. I never asked Ian
and Kathy why they visited – there was little enough
reward from seeing my father in the last year or so – but
my father had defended Ian when he was being attacked
during some of the scandals that have beset his career. Ian
remembered him being friendly when he was a 15-year-old
at Somerset, and I guess Ian is just a loyal man.

Towards the end my father sat at the end of the dining
table in depressed quietness, eyes restless but dull, a
wheelchair in the corner of the room. Talking was difficult
because of his bronchitis and his depression, and any
conversation would be linked to the nebuliser machine for
his chest or whether it was time to take his pills. Worse
still, he seemed never to get even a wicked sparkle out of
the endless series of chores he would demand from Pat or
his nurse June.

Graham Stirling told us that my father so panted for
breath because of his enormous drive. He said that frequently with patients in such a condition the brain gets
tired of sending out messages to the lungs to push so hard
for breath, and they are admitted to hospital because the
lungs are reluctant to continue the struggle. This had
never happened with my father. At the end the personality
had gone and just that incessant survival drive was left.

On Friday 13 December 1991, only a week after I had
last seen my father, my brother Robert called me at my
home in Paris to say that he had a chest infection, one lung
was blocked solid, and Struan Robertson, his Alderney
doctor, did not think he would last the next forty-eight
hours. 'He's surprised me often enough before,' Struan had
told Pat and my brother, 'but this time I don't think he
will.'

His general condition was so wretched that it was highly
likely he would die. As I caught the only direct flight from
Paris to Jersey for at least the third 'last night' at his

bedside, I still thought he would have the last laugh on his surrounding family and doctors, but I was not taking any chances. The flight schedule left me stranded on Guernsey, but Geoff Rennard, who had been living in the house for a while helping Pat take the strain of looking after my father, found someone to fetch me in a motor launch. It was as well Geoff organised the boat.

It got in shortly before midnight. A nurse called Mandy was watching my father during the night. Showing her experience with dying patients, I realised later, she spoke to my father sharply as I entered the bedroom: 'John, your son Tim's arrived from Paris.'

His eyes had been closed, but to my surprise he pulled himself up in the bed immediately – something he had not been able to do without help for a long time – and opened his eyes. I could not make out much of what he was trying to say, but I told him I would be back in a couple of minutes to say goodnight. I came back with Robert. He put one hand in each of ours and said, 'I love you.' I still thought he might last a few more days at least, but he knew better.

The nurse came upstairs to break the news about 6 a.m. He had given a cough about an hour earlier and stopped breathing.

Sitting in my place on the left of his chair at the head of the enormous dining table during the following days – reading memories, quotes and observations in every newspaper, most of them from friends who had sat many times at the same table – I found the image of a depressed man with broken health and dull and restless eyes being challenged by another memory. No, at the head of the table was a sharp-eyed, vigorous, beguiling man, who would explain his beliefs with thunderous clarity and sincerity; produce an apt and thought-provoking quotation that no listener had heard before; listen to a guest, eyes agleam with interest and concentration; tell a tale that brought uproarious laughter; or simply hold a dining-table or a radio audience in the palm of his descriptive hand. The Master. We will never know his like again.

Index

219